THE
FIVE-TOOL
PLAYER

BECOME THE TOTAL PACKAGE THAT PRO AND COLLEGE BASEBALL SCOUTS WANT

MARK GOLA

New York   Chicago   San Francisco   Lisbon   London   Madrid   Mexico City
Milan   New Delhi   San Juan   Seoul   Singapore   Sydney   Toronto

Library of Congress Cataloging-in-Publication Data

Gola, Mark.
    The five-tool player : become the total package that pro and college baseball scouts
want / Mark Gola.
        p.   cm.
    Includes index.
    ISBN 0-07-147621-0
    1. Baseball—Scouting—United States.   I. Title.

GV880.22G65   2007
796.357023—dc22
                            2006027125

1 2 3 4 5 6 7 8 9 10 11 12 13 14 15 16 17 18 19 DOC/DOC 0 9 8 7

ISBN-13: 978-0-07-147621-8
ISBN-10:   0-07-147621-0

Interior photographs by Michael Plunkett

McGraw-Hill books are available at special quantity discounts to use as premiums and sales
promotions, or for use in corporate training programs. For more information, please write
to the Director of Special Sales, Professional Publishing, McGraw-Hill, Two Penn Plaza, New
York, NY 10121-2298. Or contact your local bookstore.

This book is printed on acid-free paper.

*In loving memory of Denise Marie Lugar—
for what you've meant to my life yesterday,
today, and tomorrow*

Contents

Foreword

The baseball world defines a *five-tool player* as one who can hit for average, run, field, throw, and hit for power. Sounds very basic, yet there are so few players who can actually be called a five-tool player. Baseball is a team game defined by a very unique set of individual skills. In *The Five-Tool Player*, author Mark Gola has defined what these tools are, their role in the game of baseball, and how one can go about improving each of these skills to become the best ballplayer he can possibly become. Gola gives an in-depth analysis of each, explaining the basics and proper mechanics required to better one's game. In addition, he provides detailed programs for strength training, speed and agility work, and plyometric exercises so that players can develop into quicker, more explosive athletes.

As Gola states, "Baseball is a sport that entertains a high rate of failure . . . and it's important that players have the ability to contribute in more than one way." The more proficient a player is in all facets of the game, the more valuable a commodity he becomes to his team, coach, or organization. Baseball rosters are made up of finite numbers, and the greater the number of ways a player can contribute, the more likely that player will make a roster and see playing time. An evaluator sees the "good glove/no-hit" infielder as an offensive liability. The power hitter who strikes out more often than he makes contact entertains a limited role on anyone's team. Complete players have the ability to contribute on both sides of the ball on a daily basis.

Few people have been blessed with the skills with which to compete at the major league level, and even fewer yet have been able to earn the moniker of a five-tool player. As an evaluator at the professional level, I have found complete players to be extremely rare. When found, the complete player is fun to watch and a joy to scout. Even more fun is to see a player blessed with those skills who is driven, who plays the game with enthusiasm and a bounce in his step, and who appreciates his abilities and uses them to his highest levels on the playing field.

While physical tools are extremely important in projecting whether a player will be successful at the professional level, they are no guarantee. The player must be able to take those tools and make them usable; that is, the skills somehow must translate into success on the diamond. There are also numerous other factors an evaluator must consider when predicting a player's future: the player's heart, desire, drive, instincts, and intelligence, just to name a few. Along with physical tools, these intangibles contribute to a player's success or failure. Being successful at the high school or college level is no guarantee of success at the professional level. However, having physical tools and being unsuccessful at those levels is a pretty good indicator that the failures will continue in pro ball. I might add that it is equally important to be a good self-evaluator. You must be able to understand where your strengths and weaknesses as a player lie and how to tailor your game to them.

Certain people are blessed with god-given abilities, such as those who can run like Jose Reyes or throw like Vladimir Guerrero. Most of us weren't allotted those abilities and have had to work and hone them to perfection over years and years of repetitive training in order to advance to and compete at the highest levels of sport. *The Five-Tool Player* will help players of any age and skill level not only to improve upon the things they do well but to recognize and get better at the deficient parts of their games. It is a step-by-step, easy-to-read breakdown of what it takes to become a complete, five-tool player. Not only does this book provide you with information and guidance toward developing all aspects of your game, but I think you'll enjoy reading it as well. Players are always looking for an edge, and there's no question that knowledge is power.

CHRIS PITTARO
DIRECTOR OF PRO SCOUTING,
OAKLAND ATHLETICS

Preface

When Mark Weinstein, senior editor at McGraw-Hill, called me with his idea to develop a book titled *The Five-Tool Player*, I thought about the different ways to approach the treatment. Should the book be advanced instruction and focus on higher-level technique along with the mental and emotional aspect of performing? Would it be better to target physical conditioning and concentrate on strength, agility, and speed training? Or should the primary purpose of the treatment be to educate aspiring players on how college recruiters and professional scouts evaluate and assess talent?

Because I could envision each of the three treatments as being both interesting and informative, the solution was simple. Let's have it all. If the title is one that reflects a complete baseball player, then the book itself should be complete.

The Five-Tool Player is a book that guides players toward becoming complete baseball players. It is packed with basic and advanced information that will improve a player's physical, mental, and emotional approach to the game. A five-tool player is an individual who possesses exceptional talent in each of the five primary baseball skills by which players are assessed: hitting for average, hitting for power, defense, arm strength, and speed. This book focuses on developing and/or improving each tool.

The treatment is divided into six chapters. The first chapter discusses how each of the five tools helps a player's game, the value of versatility, the significance of self-assessment, and the importance of having short-term versus long-term goals, and it gives a brief introduction to each of the five tools. In addition, there is discussion on how college recruiters and professional scouts evaluate talent. Because many players aspire to play baseball after high school, it's important that they understand what coaches and scouts are searching for in prospective players.

Each of the remaining five chapters features an individual tool. Basic and advanced techniques are provided in every chapter. For example, in Chapter 2, "Hitting for Average," the fundamentals of the swing are broken down step-by-step, but there is also discussion on how the swing adjusts to inside, outside, high, and low strikes. Fielding a routine ground ball is understood at most levels, but how does a shortstop glove a ground ball when executing a double-play feed to second base or fielding a slow roller in the infield? Players realize that when throwing the ball, keeping the elbow above the shoulder is going to supply the best velocity and carry on the ball. But there are also times when an infielder needs to drop down and throw sidearm to get rid of the ball in a timely fashion. The rudimentary skills of the game are essential at every level of play, but this book focuses greater attention on the advanced plays and techniques.

In addition to physical instruction, the mental and emotional aspects of play are addressed. In Chapter 3, "Hitting for Power," one of the primary components featured is attitude. A player can have a strong body and great technique, but if he fails to step up to the plate and swing the bat with attitude, he's not going to realize his true power. Having a definitive plan at the plate, observing the surrounding elements to better position oneself in the field, and understanding the opposition's strengths and weaknesses are topics discussed that assist player development.

The standards by which tools are assessed accompany each chapter. Comments from college coaches and professional scouts shed light on what is considered average, above average, or below average. Some skill evaluations, like hitting and arm strength, are more subjective, while a catcher's pop-to-pop time and timing runners with a stopwatch are clear-cut.

Lastly, a more modernized approach to developing baseball players is featured. Strength, speed, agility, and plyometric training help good athletes evolve into complete baseball players. Baseball is a sport that requires a series of short, explosive movements, and there is no question that a stronger, faster, well-conditioned athlete can execute baseball skills in a manner that will enhance individual performance.

More than 100 stop-action photographs illustrate the text. The photos supply the reader with a visual image to better absorb the subject matter being discussed.

It is understood that some physical talents are god-given. Physiological makeup is a contributing component to power, bat speed, arm speed, running speed, and so on. Some players simply have a greater number of fast-twitch muscles firing in certain regions of their bodies. But the purpose of this book is to take whatever ability is given and make it better through training, technique, knowledge, and instinct.

To those who read this book, there is excellent information throughout the forthcoming pages, but it only offers value if you put it to use. Use it for selfish reasons and make yourself better. Don't be naive and think you've mastered the game, because the moment you let up, other players will pass you, and the speed of the game itself will swallow you whole.

Books, parents, and coaches can guide you and share advice, but the destiny of your career rests solely in your hands. How good you become is completely up to you and no one else. For those of you who are true competitors, I don't think you'd want it any other way.

And one final point: It takes no talent to hustle.

Acknowledgments

There are many people who made personal contributions to this publication. To all of those who helped me, I'd like to say, "Thanks."

Mark Weinstein, senior editor at McGraw-Hill, for creating the concept for this book and for your editorial contributions. Also, a special thanks to Ron Martirano at McGraw-Hill.

Michael Plunkett, photographer and friend, for taking all the great action photos that illustrate the text.

Craig Bolt, project editor at McGraw-Hill, for supervising the design and layout of the pages that bring the text and photos to life.

Randy Voorhees, the best of friends and a great baseball mind. Thanks for your thoughts throughout this project.

Dave Gallagher, my friend and boss, for your thoughts and stories, which helped spice up the text.

Two young studs—excuse me: students—Matt Hohmann and Joe Quinones, for your participation in modeling for the photo shoot. You have bright futures ahead of you.

The baseball experts who granted their time and thoughts to the treatment: George Horton, Cal State University, Fullerton head baseball coach; Richard Rembielak, Wake Forest University head baseball coach; Steve Smith, Baylor University head baseball coach; Scott Bradley, Princeton University head baseball coach; Chris Pittaro, Oakland Athletics director of pro scouting; John Wilson, Minnesota Twins scout; and Mike Garlotti, Colorado Rockies scout.

Kike Enderle, Hopewell Valley Central High School director of athletics, for use of the athletic fields for the photo shoot and for your friendship.

Jason Steinert, good friend and college teammate, for coming through with a clutch hit when I needed a movie quote from *Bull Durham*.

Dave Norris, lifelong friend, for your enthusiasm and support when it comes to book projects and always trying to make me think I'm better than I am.

Matt Golden, friend and fellow coach, for your suggestions in Chapter 5, "Arm Strength."

As always, my parents, Edward and Paulette Gola; brother, Ed Gola; and baseball coaches Stan Davis (Hopewell Valley) and Sonny Pittaro (Rider University).

1
A Complete Baseball Player

In baseball, players are often classified by the skill that makes them exceptional. A ballplayer may be identified as an outstanding hitter, a versatile defensive specialist, or a player with great speed. They earn their reputation and are revered for the special talent that makes them stand out: a great arm, a powerful bat, soft hands.

These labels are flattering, but they all fall short of the title a player should aspire to assume. The greatest compliment an individual can receive on the baseball diamond is that he's a great baseball player. It lacks glitter, but it speaks volumes.

Rather than distinguishing one skill from another, this description—being considered a great baseball player—applies to a player who can hit for average, hit for power, field, throw, and run. Such a player is complete and excels in every phase of the game. Great hitters, fielders, and runners can contribute. Great players are talked about before, during, and after the game.

In today's game, a great baseball player is known as a *five-tool player.* It's a title used to describe the elite, such as Andruw Jones, Vladimir Guerrero, Alex Rodriguez, and Carlos Beltran. A player boasting the five coveted tools on the baseball field possesses the following skills:

- He hits for average.
- He hits for power.
- He has exceptional defensive ability.
- He has a strong throwing arm.
- He has great speed.

All baseball players perform these skills, but very few do so at the highest level. Most successful players are equipped with a few of these tools, but only the especially gifted hold a five of a kind.

This book is designed to teach ballplayers how they can develop into a complete baseball player. The five tools represent the most important physical skills on the diamond. By developing and/or improving each of these tools, players will better their performance, increase their value in the eyes of respected coaches and recruiters, and heighten their chances of advancing in the game.

The Value of Possessing Five Tools

The ultimate goal for every kid who laces up the spikes should be to become a great baseball player. Players should never relegate themselves to being only a power hitter, a fielder who can really pick it, or someone with a great arm. The objective is to be really good at everything, because a complete baseball player can help a team in so many different ways. Coaches hold these players in the highest regard.

A potent bat provides a player with options if he can match it with other tools.

Baseball is a sport that entertains a high rate of failure. Players go through periods of time when they struggle at the plate, in the field, or on the base paths. Because baseball humbles its participants, it's important that players have the ability to contribute in more than one way. If a player on offense fails to drive in a runner in scoring position, he can make a fine defensive play that stops an opposing base runner from scoring. Whether you put a run on the scoreboard or take one off of your opponents, you're helping your team's chance of winning. Five-tool players aren't necessarily firing on all cylinders at all times, but they have a greater chance of producing in a game in some capacity because they are multifaceted. As 1979 National League MVP Keith Hernandez once said, "I can win a game with my glove just as easy as I can with my bat."

When a player is one-dimensional, his value (and playing time) becomes vulnerable. If hitting is his lone strength, he is of little service to his team amidst a slump. The coach or manager is now faced with the decision of possibly benching this player for someone else

To make difficult plays in the game, a player
must tackle tough plays in practice.

who has a chance of producing offensively but will certainly provide
solid defense or a baserunning threat.

"In baseball, there are fewer mistakes made at each level of the
game," says Chris Pittaro, director of pro scouting for the Oakland
Athletics. "Even in professional baseball, the mistakes made from
single-A to double-A to triple-A become less evident. So if you do
have a weakness as a player, it will be exposed at some point. You
may get away with certain things at a lower level, but as you advance,
you'll eventually reach a point where someone will say, 'This just
isn't going to cut it.' "

A Good Five Makes a Great One

All five tools are somewhat intertwined when it comes to performance on the baseball field. Each individual tool can be of benefit to
several other tools and improve your total package. Conversely, one
tool that is weak can adversely affect a different tool and reduce your
worth. Following are some examples that will explain this point.

A shortstop may have an exceptional glove, agility, and range.
Quickness and glove work may enable him to cleanly field balls that

most shortstops would fail to reach. The question is, does he have the arm strength to record the out? If so, he's a great shortstop. If not, he's an average shortstop who gets to a lot of balls. Chances are, if his arm strength is a concern, he'll have to play shallower to shorten his throw. This will cut down his range, which was his original strength.

A slower shortstop with a great arm can afford to play a little deeper to increase his range. In this case, one tool helps mask a weakness. The efforts for this player would be best spent working on improving foot speed and agility.

A power hitter is known as someone who hits the ball great distances, resulting in extra-base hits and home runs. But having power also helps your batting average. Hitting the ball with power means hitting the ball hard. The harder a hitter strikes the ball, the faster the ball leaves the bat (exit velocity speed). This gives defensive players less time to react, resulting in more hits for the batter. So a player who hits for average will become even more effective if he adds strength.

Speed out of the batter's box is going to help a hitter's average and power numbers. Speed is one tool that enhances several others.

Willie Mays—The Original Five-Tool Player

Hall of Fame manager Leo Durocher was known for his brash, fiery approach to managing baseball teams. As a player for the St. Louis Cardinals, he was a member of the infamous Gas House Gang. Never one to hold back from expressing his thoughts, Durocher had this to say in describing near-perfection on the diamond:

> *If someone came up and hit .450, stole 100 bases and performed a miracle in the field every day, I'd still look you in the eye and say Willie [Mays] was better. He could do the five things you have to do to be a superstar: hit, hit for power, run, throw, and field. And he had that other magic ingredient that runs a superstar into a super superstar. He lit up the room when he came in. He was a joy to be around.*

Whether it be through the written word or discussions with players from the past or present, the name Willie Mays is synonymous with the term *five-tool player*. His baseball talents are the measuring stick by which that type of player is defined. Hank Aaron, Roberto Clemente, Ken Griffey Jr., Vladimir Guerrero, and Alex Rodriguez are often mentioned when the five-tool topic is addressed, but none are stated with the conviction that the Mays legacy commands.

Willie Mays had it all. There was nothing he couldn't do on the baseball field. Video footage displays flashes of his brilliance, but even those clips don't give justice to how good he was day in, day out. His great speed and defensive instinct were showcased during the 1954 World Series when he outran that deep fly ball hit some 440 feet by Vic Wertz. Mays ripping a line drive to right-center field at the Polo Grounds and storming around the bases before sliding in safely for a triple is a demonstration of his multi-faceted offensive talents.

But Mays was even more than that. On the bases, he was rarely ever thrown out. He had an uncanny ability of knowing when to steal or when to take the extra base and stretch a single to a double. In addition, he used every type of slide known to man, which helped him elude tags and further frustrate his opponents.

At the plate, Mays was a nightmare for pitchers because he could beat you in so many ways. He assaulted pitches with blinding bat speed and barrel precision, which enabled him to club 660 career home runs and compile a lifetime .302 batting average. Yet Mays would drop down a drag bunt to reach base and ignite a rally. He treated each at-bat as a personal confrontation between himself and the pitcher and never allowed himself to be anything less than a tough out.

Willie Mays was a five-tool player. But what made him a legend, what makes people blurt his name out when asked to name the greatest all-around player the game has ever seen, was that he combined his athletic talents with a relentless, competitive drive. He was addicted to success. His unwillingness to lose a battle with a pitcher, his unwillingness to be thrown out on the bases, his unwillingness to let a fly ball drop safely in the outfield—that was the difference between Mays being great and being the greatest. There have been baseball players who could run as fast as Mays, who could hit the ball as far and consistently as Mays, who could play the outfield as well as Mays. But there has only been one Willie Mays.

The Say-Hey Kid's Career Achievements
.302 career batting average (including the 1954 batting title)
660 career home runs (led the NL four times)
338 stolen bases (led the NL four times)
140 career triples (led the NL three times)
.557 career slugging percentage (led the NL five times)
.387 career on-base percentage (led the NL two times)
.981 career fielding percentage
7,095 putouts (all-time career leader in outfield putouts)
12 Gold Glove Awards (Gold Gloves weren't awarded until 1957)

Speed helps a baseball player everywhere on the field. It helps him run down balls in the outfield, leg out slow rollers in the infield, score from first base on a double, or charge and throw out a runner on a chopper in the infield. Kenny Lofton, who has played in the major leagues since 1991, is a great example of an athlete whose primary baseball tool was speed and who went on to develop everything else around it. Lack of speed can be a hindrance on a player's offense and defense.

A good baseball player has skill in each of these five areas: hitting for average, hitting for power, fielding, throwing, and running. Don't make the mistake of neglecting certain tools because they seem less important. As you progress in the sport, that weakness will eventually be exposed and limit your value and performance.

> *If you're not practicing, somebody else is, somewhere, and he'll be ready to take your job.*
>
> —Brooks Robinson, Hall of Fame third baseman

Assessing Yourself as a Baseball Player

Baseball is a very tough game, and we're not all Willie Mays. Few players are as physically gifted as Mays, Griffey, Jeter, and so on. Even though major league players are extraordinarily gifted, only a small crop are considered five-tool players by major league standards. But every player can take their god-given abilities and make them better. Each tool can be assessed, developed, and improved. The objective for every player (regardless of age or ability) is to take what they have and make it better. Take the strengths and make them stronger. Take the weaknesses and strive to turn them into strengths. Enhancing strengths and eliminating weaknesses create a domino effect that not only embellishes skill but has a positive psychological impact. A player who is satisfied with his training and personal enhancement builds confidence and plays with greater presence on the field. Confidence and positive thought bring greater success. Success breeds success.

A baseball player should always be in search of how he can get better. To do so, he must address his strengths and shortcomings. This does not require an expert. It simply takes honesty and sensibility from the player himself or those surrounding him. "He can hit, but he has no defensive position." "He can run, but he lacks strength." "He's got a good bat and glove, but he has a weak throwing arm." Players know what they're good at and where they struggle, but they often avoid admitting or acknowledging weaknesses. A coach, teammate, or parent can be helpful if a player is in need of deciphering personal strengths from weaknesses. It's useful information that is not imparted to damage pride but to provide direction that leads toward improvement.

To improve at each of these tools, players must be equipped with a few components. They must develop knowledge of the skill and an understanding of how they individually perform each skill. They must design a plan to improve and commit to executing that plan.

There are also players out there who have great talent but fail to put forth the effort to reach their potential. Baseball is a highly skilled game of routine and repetition. To optimize performance and play in a relaxed, composed state, players must practice the skills of the game. As the late Charlie Lau once noted, "Nothing is more common than unsuccessful men with talent."

If outfield defense is an aspect of a player's game that needs work, he must dedicate more time in practice to improve those skills.

Goal Setting

Setting goals is helpful in player development, but there must be a combination of short-term goals and long-term goals. Long-term goals are simple. What is it that you hope to achieve? The most common answer is to become a major league baseball player. OK, it's a lofty goal, but there are hundreds of players who achieve that goal every year. Just understand that the realistic chances of making it that far are slim. Some players aspire to one day sign a professional baseball contract, play collegiate baseball, make their high school varsity team, play middle school ball with their classmates, or play travel baseball with friends. There is no right or wrong answer. Personal objectives can be different for everyone, and if those objectives are achieved, the individual can set a new, long-term goal.

Short-term goals direct players how to get better now and pave the way toward achieving their long-term goals. A short-term goal might be, for example, an infielder getting better at charging balls and throwing on the run. A hitter may work toward improvement on handling low strikes. A base runner may focus on polishing his running form and making better turns on the base paths. A player should use the five tools as a guide, isolate an area of each that needs personal improvement, and use these areas as the focal point of his

Improving upon double-play feeds from shortstop is a short-term goal that may help foster long-term success.

practice. Eliminating these areas of weakness immediately makes the player better and brings him closer to his long-term goal.

A mistake players make is that they focus on the long-term goal and forget to set short-term goals. They fail to address their needs and instead spend their time talking about wanting to play at the next level. The levels at which you'll play will take care of itself. If you attend to your own needs and exercise the desire to develop each of the five tools, you will scale the wall and play at the highest level you're capable of playing. Even better than that, you will enhance your success and enjoyment playing the game.

Developing the Five Tools

Every tool in your personal arsenal must be targeted, and the purpose of evaluating the state of your game is to earmark what you do well and what needs the most work. All of the tools will be targeted, but the efforts placed on each tool will be based on need.

This point brings us to an unfortunate trend that is practiced by many players. Simply stated, players do not like to practice their areas of weakness. They would rather stick with what they do well. There is no question that it's fun to work on the things that come easily. It takes less effort and concentration, and the results are more rewarding. The skills of the game that don't come so easily bring frustration. The game's no longer fun—it seems like work. But this is where you get better. These are the areas that offer the biggest jump in enhancing your game.

Let's take hitting for average and discuss a quick example. A hitter may determine that he absolutely crushes pitches middle-in and down in the strike zone. He might say, "If the ball is thrown in that zone, the pitcher is in serious trouble." That's all good, and it's also important knowledge for when you're hitting early or ahead in the count. But the better question to ask yourself is, "If I were pitching against myself, how would I pitch me?" Sounds odd, but it provides useful information. "I'd target the outside part of the plate or throw pitches up in the strike zone." Right there, a hitter has mapped out details to a plan toward becoming a better hitter. He should work on pitches away and up in the strike zone. If he becomes more proficient at handling those areas, he's a more rounded hitter and a tougher out.

Players should also avoid taking on an over-specific identity at a young age and accepting that player classification. Too often players pigeonhole themselves by position, for example, claiming, "I'm a first baseman," or "Catching is the only position I'll ever play," or the most popular declaration, "I only play shortstop." Why limit yourself to a single position on the field? At some point, individuals will encounter a teammate who plays the same position. And guess what? He might be better. Now the first player is relegated to the bench because he has no real playing experience anywhere else on the field.

This point is not meant to dissuade players from having a primary position; however, they should seek practice and game time developing secondary positions. Specializing in one spot on the field is

An infielder must be the best at his position in order to crack the starting lineup. An outfielder needs to be in the top three to be a starter.

shortsighted and may present a roadblock down the line. And please, at a young age don't ever declare yourself as a designated hitter. The life of your baseball career will be reduced significantly. "A player who has versatility is extremely important to a college coach," says Steve Smith, head baseball coach at Baylor University. "It's important to me primarily due to scholarship and roster limitations."

The skills you emphasize when evaluating a prospect vary by position. When looking at a catcher you're looking at his hands and feet . . . the strength of his arm. Basically you're looking at his defensive skills first, much like you do with a shortstop. If it's a corner position [first and third] or a corner outfielder, the emphasis is placed more on offense. How the physical tools apply and how important they are depends on the position they play.

—John Wilson, area scout, Minnesota Twins

Ranking Tools by Position

All five tools are important to being a well-rounded baseball player; however, certain tools have greater significance to recruiters and scouts depending on the player's position. Following is a chart of how major league organizations typically rank the importance of each tool by each position.
Key: 1=field; 2=throw; 3=bat; 4=power; 5=run

Position	Order of Rank
Catcher	1, 2, 3, 4, 5
First base	3, 4, 1, 2, 5
Second base	3, 1, 5, 4, 2
Shortstop	1, 2, 5, 3, 4
Third base	3, 4, 1, 2, 5
Left field	3, 4, 5, 1, 2
Center field	5, 1, 3, 2, 4
Right field	3, 4, 1, 2, 5

The five chapters that follow this one provide detail toward developing the five tools. Review each chapter thoroughly. There will be information of use even if you consider yourself a master of a particular tool. Also, each chapter will provide information on how professional scouts and college recruiters assess each tool. The next five sections offer brief introductions to the remaining chapters.

Hitting for Average

Hitting for a high batting average is never accomplished by accident. It is achieved through observation, experience, practice, and yes, failure. Young players may enjoy hitting success at the rudimentary levels of play, but as they advance, it gets much more difficult. The good news is that hitting for high average is one of the tools that requires the least god-given talent. Technique, intelligence, the ability to make adjustments, and work ethic are necessary traits for this tool, none of which are completely dependent on genetics.

Consistency is integral to hitting for a high average. Becoming a consistent hitter takes more than boasting a fundamentally sound swing. Of course, having solid mechanics and an understanding of your own swing is important, but that is just a piece of the puzzle. Hitters must achieve full plate coverage (hit all locations of the strike zone) and develop the ability to hit to all fields. They must build a personal approach to hitting and be able to adjust that approach when factoring in recent personal successes or failures, the game situation, and the pitcher's patterns of attack. Hitters must understand their strengths and weaknesses, their personal hitting zone, and common faults in their swing. Hitters must never get too high or too low with their emotions. These are all necessary components to becoming a consistent hitter.

Acquiring these traits is not enough. They must be conditioned. Habitual physical and mental preparation is essential. When a player has taken the time to polish his swing and digs his feet in the batter's box with a definitive plan, he will feel prepared. This raises his level of confidence, which enhances performance. These topics and several others are addressed in Chapter 2.

Players who hit for high average are able to drive balls in all areas of the strike zone. Here, the hitter raises his hands to level off on a high strike.

Hitting for Power

Striking the baseball solid and sending it prodigious distances is a tasty reward for the batter, but it does not define a power hitter. Hitting for power requires strength, technique, fearlessness, and attitude (presence at the plate). A hitter who carries his bat with attitude is one who instills concern in the mind of the pitcher.

A stronger athlete is a better athlete. It's a fact that is indisputable. Does strength alone make a hitter a power hitter? Absolutely not. But take a good hitter and add strength, and his performance will improve. There are sports-specific muscle regions for baseball players to target; they will be outlined in Chapter 3.

In the 1970s Ted Williams documented his philosophy on rotational hitting. During the 1980s Charlie Lau became famous in baseball circles for his ideology on weight-shift hitting. Each of these philosophies will be examined, but to maximize power in every swing, a hitter must employ a combination of both. There is no question that rotating the hips generates power from the lower half of the body; however, a degree of weight shift must also occur to manifest every ounce of strength through the baseball.

Hitting the ball with power entails strength, quickness, balance, and tenacity.

The mind-set of a power hitter is critical to performance. The right mental attitude can be transferred into better bat speed. Rather than attempting to hit the ball, power hitters look to attack the ball, to assault the incoming pitch and drive through the baseball. Many hitters stand in the batter's box attempting to make contact, and if that is their approach, that is pretty much what they'll do—make contact. But that's all they'll do. Power hitters are unafraid to swing and miss, because they accept that without some degree of risk, there is no major reward.

Defense

Learning to play all of the defensive positions is in the best interest of a young baseball player. It helps the player to develop the full spectrum of defensive skills and also makes him more knowledgeable. By understanding the nuances of each position, players become more instinctive and better able to anticipate.

Identifying a primary position requires sensibility and honesty. Players must attempt to match a position that best suits their individual talents and avoids exploiting their shortcomings. Assessing the skills of need at each position will be discussed in Chapter 4. For their primary position, a left-hander, for example, should stick with first base, pitching, or the outfield positions. It doesn't mean they can never play anywhere else in early stages in their careers, but they will be limited to those spots as they progress.

Like hitting, playing good defense has many elements. Technique is essential to playing consistently; it's built through repetitious training. Understanding personal strengths and weaknesses provides focus for practice sessions and improvement. Lastly, good defensive players *want* the ball to be hit to them every time. If that is not the case, the player is not whole and has a lot of work ahead of him.

Good defensive players are valued because they take runs off the scoreboard, which is just as good as tacking them on.

Arm Strength

Physiological makeup is a factor in arm strength. Can Josh Beckett explain exactly why he can throw a ball 98 miles per hour? Probably not. Are technique and work ethic the reasons why Roberto Clemente could stand at the center field wall and throw a ball on a straight line to home plate? No. Genetics had something to do with that as well. How fast a player can accelerate his throwing arm forward depends somewhat on god-given ability.

That being said, each player's arm strength can stand to improve. There are players who have good arms but flawed throwing mechanics. Detecting and correcting those glitches in the delivery will improve arm strength and throwing accuracy. Plenty of players have great throwing fundamentals but simply don't throw enough. They fail to condition their arms and maximize the velocity and carry of their throws.

A player with a strong, accurate throwing arm can force opposing teams to run the bases conservatively, which helps keep runs off the scoreboard.

The mechanics of the throw will be reviewed in detail in Chapter 5. Position players often pay little attention to throwing technique, assuming that's a topic of interest for pitchers only. Throwing the ball properly optimizes velocity, carry (how far a ball travels true through the air), and accuracy. It also minimizes the risk of arm soreness and injury.

The value in having arm strength on the field is more than just recording outs. It's also about gaining respect from the opponent. A catcher with a great arm may shut down a team's running game without even throwing out a base runner. An outfielder with a strong arm can keep a team from taking extra bases without even recording an outfield assist. Good arms on defense force opponents to run the bases more conservatively.

Players who have limited arm strength must figure out alternate methods of proving their worth on the field. They need to cheat and anticipate the play. Those who are attentive on defense absorb available information and put that knowledge to use to position themselves and anticipate. Improving speed and agility and quickening the release of throws are also skills that help overcome mediocre arm strength. These topics will be addressed.

Speed

There is no other skill that players give up on quicker than running speed and/or general baserunning. Speed is also the lone tool that helps players on both sides of the ball (offense and defense). Players tend to accept the fact that they're slow-footed and fail to work on this part of their game. This is a colossal mistake. Whether a player can progress from slow to adequate speed, adequate to good speed, or good to great speed, he needs to improve this area of his game.

You don't have to be fast to be a good base runner. And with that, fast runners are not necessarily good base runners. Anticipation, observation, and knowing your opponents are important factors in being a good base runner. Running good angles and making efficient turns are elements of great significance.

Speed is a tool that enhances or diminishes two other tools: playing defense and hitting for average. You could make a case for arm

Speed on the base paths is disruptive to the pitcher and infielders.

strength, because if you can't get to the ball in a timely fashion, you won't have the opportunity to show off your arm.

Running form will be discussed along with speed, agility, and plyometric training in Chapter 6. Playing baseball requires skills based largely on a series of short, explosive movements; players will benefit from a comprehensive training program.

How Pro Scouts Evaluate Players

The purpose of this book is to help baseball players assess themselves and further develop each of the five tools. It is in no way a guarantee that a player will end up playing professional baseball. There are too many factors involved to consider that a probability. That being said, ballplayers are recommended to make long-term goals,

A Sharp Tool May Dull in Comparison at the Next Level

Continue to work on improving your tools, even the ones you might consider your greatest strength. You may be a big fish in a small pond and eventually realize there is an ocean of talent out there.

Dave Gallagher was a major league outfielder for nine years. He was drafted twice as a first-round draft pick out of Mercer County Community College before signing his first pro contract. Gallagher was a very good hitter and an exceptional outfielder. His running speed was a big part of his game, aiding him at the plate, in the outfield, and on the bases.

After experiencing several successful years in the minor leagues, Gallagher was invited to major league spring training with the Chicago White Sox. He was competing for the center field position with Dwight Taylor. Taylor was not a polished baseball player, but he had phenomenal speed. Gallagher quickly discovered that one of his greatest strengths no longer gave him an edge at the major league level.

"They were basically looking for reasons to keep Dwight and give him the center field position," Gallagher recalls. "It was ironic for me because speed had been a tool that fueled my game, and now it was my nemesis. The organization felt his speed was so extraordinary, they would give him time to develop the other parts of his game. Because I couldn't compete with his speed, I had to overwhelm the big league club with the other tools. I was a much stronger hitter than him, possessed a better throwing arm, and had good baseball instincts. Although he could outrun me, I anticipated the game and took better angles on the bases and in the outfield. Fortunately, I did enough of everything to win the job. His one tool [speed] was incredible, but he didn't have enough to contribute day in and day out at that level."

with professional baseball (ultimately, the major leagues) being the grand prize. It is not only intriguing but also beneficial for amateur players to understand what professional scouts look for in pro prospects and how they measure talent. Each chapter forthcoming will address what makes a professional scout label a prospective player as possessing the particular tool discussed in that chapter.

The job of a professional scout is a difficult one. In some respects, scouts are prognosticators. They must predict or project how much a player will develop in the near and distant future, how he will perform against competition that is far superior to what he's currently opposing, and how he will respond to the pressures of playing professional baseball. To watch a 17-year-old play a high school baseball game and project whether that player will eventually have the physical tools and mental makeup to play major league baseball years down the road is a pretty tall task.

One of the first assessments a scout makes is whether the player has a passion to play baseball or if he simply enjoys it because it's something he's good at. When a player signs a professional contract, baseball becomes his livelihood. It becomes his life. There are no fancy cars, high-rise suites, or flying first-class in minor league baseball. The money is sparse, the bus rides are long, and players rent small apartments with their teammates. A player must love playing the sport and be determined to work at it in order to survive the rigors of minor league baseball. Signing a player who is only interested in the sport because he's always played it and sees potential dollar signs is a mistake. That type of motivation is not enough for a player to withstand the peaks and valleys of a professional career.

It doesn't take very long for professional scouts to determine whether a player is prideful in his play and passionate about the sport. They observe a player during pregame and in infield/outfield practice. They watch how he takes the field, what he does between pitches, where his eyes are looking when he's on the bench awaiting his at-bats, and how he interacts with teammates. The little things tell a lot about a player and whether he's worthy of employment.

Assessing talent is subjective. One scout may believe that a particular player is a major league prospect, and another scout standing right next to him may cross that player's name off of his list. Major league organizations have different philosophies and opinions on the type of talent required to play major league baseball. Although there is no perfect science or formula that scouts all agree upon in assessing talent, there are general observations and opinions that most scouts would consider accurate.

If I think a player is a real prospect, I'll find out as much as I can about him. I'll actually go to their football or basketball games in the off-season to see what kind of competitor they are, if they're tough, if they have good leadership skills. You don't always see everything in a baseball game. I like to see them in situations where they succeed and fail to get a true measure of what their makeup is like.

—Mike Garlotti, area scout, Colorado Rockies

Scouts and college coaches like to see infielders throw from deep shortstop to gauge their arm strength, ball flight, and carry across the infield.

The five tools provide a basic foundation of what scouts are looking for in a prospect. Does this hitter have power? What is his barrel accuracy like? How much ground does the center fielder cover, and what is his speed like on the bases? Is the arm strength of the right fielder considered above average at the professional level? Does the shortstop have the ability to field through the ball and throw the ball with velocity on the run? These are general questions that scouts seek to answer when watching a player.

Interested parties also often misconstrue what a scout is focusing on when watching a player. Scouts are primarily evaluating a player's actions, not the final results. In other words, if a hitter goes 3-for-4 in a game and his teammate goes 0-for-3, it doesn't mean the player with three hits will earn a better scouting report than the one with no hits. Scouts are looking at the hitter's hand action (bat speed), balance, size and strength, quickness, barrel accuracy, and so on. Statistics are an additive when evaluating and projecting talent. They are not the meat and potatoes (substance) of how a scout judges a player.

"I think most people misconceive the importance of performance when it comes to evaluating talent," explains Chris Pittaro, director of pro scouting for the Oakland Athletics. "I'll get calls after the draft from people who can't believe their son didn't get drafted despite hitting .500 in high school. But we're evaluating things like balance, hand speed, strength, ability to recognize pitches, etc., and projecting whether those traits are good enough to succeed at a higher level of play. Pitchers have greater velocity, sharper breaking pitches, and better command. All of the fielders behind that pitcher are professionals, so a lot of those hits in high school become outs. It's tough to project and there are times that we're wrong, but we're looking at a player in terms of what he'll do down the road, not necessarily what he's done to this point."

Pro scouts use a 20–80 scale (some use 2–8) to grade each of the tools. Neither extreme is given very often, but professional players will typically have at least one tool rating that is very high. In other words, a baseball person will be able to look at a pro player and say, "That's why he's here." But the true prospects have several tools that are rated above-average to outstanding by major league standards.

Ratings (by major league standards) are typically scored in the following fashion:

70–80   Well above average; all-star
60–69   Above average
50–59   Major league average
40–49   Below average; fringe player (skill)
30–39   Well below average
20–29   Not a prospect

Following is a sample scouting grade of a player who is a minor league center fielder:

Hitting: 60 (above average)
Power: 45 (below average)
Fielding: 55 (average to above average)
Arm: 50 (average)
Speed: 65 (well above average)

College Recruiters

College coaches are evaluating players in a similar fashion with regard to talent, but in many ways, their search is more defined. First, they are projecting whether a player is talented enough to play collegiate baseball, rather than professional baseball. It is more manageable to determine how a player will progress over the next one to four years. Many talented high school players are capable of competing at the college level while they're still playing scholastic baseball.

Timing plays a larger role in being recruited for college programs. Recruiters are seeking players based on their program's specific need. For example, a university may be graduating four pitchers, two middle infielders, and a catcher. In this case, the school would be looking for players to fill those positions. Other roles such as leadoff hitter, left-handed power hitter, closer, or utility player are on a coach's wish list. If a player is talented and can fill a hole for that college program, he may gain interest.

It works to the disadvantage of a player who wishes to join a program that is overloaded in that position. A player may have his sights set on playing for the University of North Carolina. He is a third baseman and talented enough to play at that level. However, the Tar Heels roster includes a returning senior who is the starting third baseman, as well as a sophomore backup third baseman and a freshman infielder who is capable of playing third base. For that recruiting year, UNC coaches would likely have little interest in recruiting a third baseman.

Other factors also come into play, such as a player's attitude, work ethic, and behavior off the field. Academics, however, are essential. Players must be committed to the fact that they are attending college to earn a degree first and that playing baseball is secondary. A high school student must meet the academic standards of the institution to gain admittance and must earn the grades to remain eligible to play. If a coach has doubts that a prospective player will be able to survive in the classroom, he will turn to another candidate.

Finally, ballplayers must take stock in whether they're sure they want to commit to playing college baseball. It is extremely time demanding and entails year-round dedication. The last thing players want to do is use baseball as the primary reason to select a col-

Even at advanced levels of play, it is critical that players are open to instruction and accept it as a means of improving their individual play.

lege and then discover they really aren't interested in committing to the sport.

We try to recruit the best baseball players. Of course, we will always welcome physical tools on top of that. I think that young men who flat out know how to play the game often have an easier transition to the college level and are able to make an immediate impact on your program.

—George Horton, Cal State University, Fullerton

Here are some misconceptions about college baseball and the recruiting process:

- **Baseball programs give out full scholarships to players they recruit.** The maximum number of scholarships that a Division I baseball program has to offer by NCAA regulation is 11.7 per year. That is for the entire team. In other words, if 9.5 scholarships are devoted to returning players, only 2.2 scholarships are available for the incoming freshman class. That is throughout the nation and includes programs like Arizona State, Miami, USC, and Texas. Some programs are not given the maximum number by their individual institutions, while others offer no baseball scholarships. Most programs carry between 26 and 32 players on the roster, so scholarship money has to be spread around. Full scholarships are a rarity in baseball and typically go to pitchers if anyone at all.
- **I want to play in the South or on the West Coast at a big-time program.** You may want to play there, but they may not need you. Players have to be realistic and try to understand how much talent is really out there. If you check their rosters, you'll see that the majority of roster players at perennial powerhouse programs are in-state residents. It doesn't mean you can't dream, but to play there it takes much more than simply wanting to. Unfortunately, good players from warm-weather states rarely want to play college baseball in a cold-weather state.

- **I'll walk on when I get there.** Most baseball programs entering the fall and spring seasons have a roster that is pretty well set with returning players and incoming freshmen recruits. Walk-on tryouts are a mere formality in most cases and last just one or two days. Coaches may only be looking to discover a diamond in the rough during walk-on tryouts.
- **I've got to play Division I baseball to play quality college baseball.** There is a lot of exceptional baseball played at the junior college, NAIA, and Division II and III levels. In fact, several Division III schools could whip up on some Division I schools. Many excellent collegiate baseball programs can be found at great academic institutions, regardless of division.
- **Since I'm really good, I don't have to worry about my grades.** The better the academic standing of a prospective collegiate athlete, the more options he gives himself. If a student is unable to meet or maintain academic requirements, the coach will simply find someone who does. Coaches do not want to be burdened with players who cause concern in the classroom.

No matter how much physical ability a player may possess, he must enjoy playing the game in order to flourish. Every now and then, it's OK to crack a smile.

In addition to physical tools, what does a player need to have to achieve success?

They need to know how to play the game. Savvy, *I believe, is the missing tool.*

> —George Horton, head baseball coach,
> Cal State University, Fullerton

A player has to have the inner drive to be the best, but more importantly, he must understand the game. A player must be able to continually make adjustments.

> —Richard Rembielak, head baseball coach,
> Wake Forest University

A player needs legitimate confidence and mental toughness to deal with failure.

> —Steve Smith, head baseball coach, Baylor University

It's critical that he plays the game relaxed. That will enable him to maintain his athleticism and efficiency on the field. I've seen thousands of players field ground balls with great technique in pregame. What I want to see is a player fielding a ground ball with a runner on third base. The player who tightens up in that situation is not going to make it.

> —Scott Bradley, former major league player and head
> baseball coach, Princeton University

There are three makeup questions that I'll try to answer when scouting a player. (1) How will he handle failure? (2) Does he have the ability to make adjustments? (3) Does he have the makeup to survive the minor leagues? The minor leagues are a tough lifestyle, and it takes mental and emotional strength to make it.

> —John Wilson, area scout, Minnesota Twins

In some respects, I think evaluating physical talent is the easy part. Sometimes what takes more work is assessing

continued

what is now being called the sixth tool: makeup. You want players to have instincts, maturity, an ability to deal with failure. . . . We'll even look into whether a player seems to be injury-prone. Not everything is based on performance.
—Mike Garlotti, area scout, Colorado Rockies

When I first look at a player, I look at his energy. I watch his body language. Does he have life? Does he hustle? Does he appear as if he really enjoys playing? Because if he doesn't, it's not a good sign. I also pay attention to how he reacts to scouts being present. Some kids see a scout and look at it as an opportunity to show off. That's a good thing. Other kids cave. If the pressure gets to him that much, how is he going to respond to thousands of people watching him as he faces talented competition?
—Chris Pittaro, director of pro scouting, Oakland Athletics

2
Hitting for Average

The type of player who hits for average falls in line with the ideology of this book. He is a *complete* hitter. Great hitters are by no means one-dimensional. When gripping the baseball bat, they are multitalented individuals. Whether a right-hander or a left-hander is on the mound, they're playing a day game or a night game, it's early in the count or there are two strikes, they're thrown an inside strike or an outside strike, the best hitters find a way to put the barrel on the ball.

When hearing the term *batting average*, we typically think of a specific number. But the term should be taken in a more literal meaning. It's a cumulative average of a player's performance at the plate. Throughout the life of a season, hitters experience hot streaks as well as periods when they slump. Good hitters are able to stretch out the good and minimize the bad. They are familiar with the word *why*: Why am I hitting the ball so well? Why am I struggling? To extend the good times and diffuse the periods of failure, hitters must take note of what is causing these patterns.

Statistics are not often a true measure of physical tools, but this tool is primarily based on numbers. Either you hit for a high average or you don't. However, that number represents a player's success for the specific level he is playing at. In other words, a hitter may be a successful hitter (bats .410) at the high school level, but that's not a guarantee he'll be a good hitter at the college level. The pri-

Great hitters are able to block out the surrounding elements and focus on one thing: the incoming pitch.

mary reason for this is that the pitching gets better. Pitchers throw harder, have a deeper arsenal of pitch types, have better command of each pitch, and throw pitches with a purpose. In addition, the defensive players become much better at each level. They possess better range and stronger arms and understand how to position themselves. A hit at one level may be an easy out at the next. Players have to earn their hits as the competition gets tougher.

As Minnesota Twins scout John Wilson explains, "Hitting is the most difficult tool to assess in my business because a high school player is facing high school pitching with average defensive players in the field. It's not what he's going to encounter in the minor leagues. Statistics have very little to do with evaluating a high school hitter, and that's a misconception a lot of people have. We look at his bat speed, the looseness of his swing, what kind of body he has, and whether he's athletic. We don't pay much attention to statistics because they're not applicable when projecting a player against better competition."

Timing and hand-eye coordination are instrumental in achieving barrel accuracy. Good hitters are consistent in getting their barrel to the middle of the baseball. It's the key to hitting the ball hard and getting hits. The very best hitters, however, are able to achieve barrel accuracy even when their timing is suspect. Part of a pitcher's plan is to disrupt the hitter's timing, and during many at-bats, they are successful in doing so. But the very best hitters can be fooled (out front) or be late starting to the ball and still figure out a way to get the barrel of the bat on the ball. That is hitting.

As Bryant Ward, Cal State, Fullerton head baseball coach, mentions, "Being that it's the pitcher's job to mess up your timing, what I think separates good hitters from great hitters is the ability to be successful when you're not on time. Those are usually the guys with great bat speed on top of great mechanics."

While hitting for average is based on statistics, there are still traits the individual must have that demonstrate he'll be successful at higher levels of play. Players should keep in mind that college recruiters and scouts must project performance at their levels. Hitters at lower levels of play who boast great statistics may get exposed against superior pitching and defense. Following is a compilation of 10 areas of hitting that professional scouts are attentive to when evaluating a hitter:

Balance
Hand-eye coordination
Bat speed
Power
Hitting to all fields
Effort level
Reaction to breaking pitches
Hitting in pressure situations
Plate discipline
Ability to make adjustments

The Three Cs of Hitting

Players who hit for high average possess three essential characteristics. They are complete, consistent, and confident. These traits are just as important as boasting a great swing.

Being a *complete* hitter means having the ability to excel under any circumstance. A complete hitter is equipped with the ability to turn on inside strikes, drive pitches on the outer half of the plate to the opposite field, go down to stroke a low strike, or raise his hands to level off on a high strike. Complete hitters can handle hard throwers as well as junk ballers. They have good plate discipline, an awareness of their hitting zone, and a workable approach to each at-bat. (These elements are further discussed later in this chapter.)

A hitter that is *consistent* with his swing, approach, and demeanor has a greater chance of hitting for a high average. Consistency affords a hitter the best opportunity to strike the middle of the ball with the barrel on a regular basis. Frequently hitting the ball hard is going to pay dividends. This is often referred to as having barrel accuracy. Regardless of pitch location, speed, or type, good hitters find a way of striking the ball with the barrel.

Inconsistent hitters are streaky. They're either hot or cold. This is not conducive to hitting for a high average because when factoring in great pitching and good defensive play, the hitter has to give himself a chance as often as possible to chalk up hits.

Perhaps the most important C of all is *confidence*. Every good hitter has confidence. The best hitters have confidence all the time, regardless of circumstance. A confident hitter who is 0-for-4 in a game is itching to get that fifth at-bat because he knows he's about to do some damage.

Confident hitters view themselves as the hunter. Hitters who lack confidence see themselves as the hunted. They're up there to survive. Confidence allows the mind and body to work at optimum levels. Thoughts are focused, the eyes pick the ball up clearly, and the body reacts in an explosive, authoritative manner. As the great and menacing hitter Ty Cobb once said, "Every great batter works on the theory that the pitcher is more afraid of him than he is of the pitcher."

A good hitter has an aura about him that emanates confidence.

The Mechanics of the Swing

Great hitters have physical, mental, and emotional abilities. Each ability serves an important purpose. Swinging the bat encompasses the physical part of hitting. It entails constant practice and understanding. In order to practice correctly and build good habits, hitters should have a general comprehension of the mechanics of the swing.

Grip and Stance

A proper grip and stance do not make a hitter, but when practiced improperly, they can break one. Gripping the bat and getting into a workable (and comfortable) batting stance are often perceived as simplistic and unimportant. This is why many swing flaws originate in these areas.

GRIP. There are three main points to remember when gripping a baseball bat:

- **The bat is gripped in the fingers, not the palms.** Strength and quickness lie in the fingers, and that is where good hitters hold the bat. There is a line created in the hand where the bottom of the fingers meets the top of the palm. This is where the handle of the bat rests. The fingers then wrap around the handle to grip the bat. This affords the hitter optimum strength, quickness, and bat control.

  A common mistake is jamming the bat back in the palm near the thumb. This occurs at an early age when hitters' hands are small and they look to the broadest surface area to hold the bat. Gripping the bat deep in the palms restricts bat speed and power. It also makes it difficult for the hitter to keep his hands in the palm-up, palm-down position through contact. He will mistakenly roll his top hand over prematurely (before contact) and hit a lot of ground balls to the pull-side.
- **The middle knuckles should be aligned or slightly off-center.** There are three sets of knuckles in the fingers: top, middle, and bottom. The middle knuckles are aligned in a proper grip. The hitter can turn his top hand so its middle knuckles are slightly

off-center (toward the bottom knuckles), but not to the point where they are aligned with the bottom knuckles.

Lining up the middle knuckles keeps the bat in the fingers and gives the swing balance, maximizing strength, quickness, and bat control. In order to have good barrel accuracy (striking the ball with the barrel of the bat), a hitter must control the head of the bat. A common mistake is to have the top-hand middle knuckles aligned with or even past the bottom knuckles. This produces a top-hand-dominant swing, which makes it difficult to take a direct path to the ball, keep the top hand from rolling over at contact, and hit to the opposite field.

- **The grip must be free of tension.** The muscles must be relaxed to be explosive. A proper grip is firm enough to hold the bat, but not so tight that the muscles in the wrists and forearms contract. Players often flick their fingers off the handle as they're awaiting the pitch, an exercise used to keep tension out of their grip.

The handle of the bat is held in the fingers, and the middle knuckles should be aligned or slightly off-center.

A grip that is too tight slows the bat. The muscles simply don't work as quickly when they're tense. The barrel will drag and the hitter will be late on pitches if he's holding the bat too tight.

STANCE—SQUARE, OPEN, CLOSED. Watch any baseball game and you'll witness at least 15 different batting stances. Albert Pujols, David Ortiz, Todd Helton, and Ichiro Suzuki are all great hitters, and each of them employs a different batting stance. There is no perfect way to stand at the plate, but there are two traits every stance must have for a hitter to experience consistent success. The hitter's stance must be *comfortable* and it must be *workable*. If either of these characteristics is missing, the stance must be adjusted.

A hitter must have comfort at the plate in order to be relaxed and self-assured. If he is standing a certain way because he was told to do so by an adult and it doesn't feel comfortable, it's not going to work. He won't believe in himself. However, the stance must also be workable. If the hitter wants to stand a certain way but continually fails as a result, he must adjust his stance. Little idiosyncrasies—holding the hands too high, tapping the front foot, rapid hand movement, standing extremely open/closed—can disrupt timing and/or place the hitter in a poor position to start his swing. Young hitters enjoy emulating players they watch on television, but a stance that works for one hitter won't necessarily bring success to another.

Listed here are a few basic checkpoints that should be evident in every batting stance:

- Feet are positioned slightly more than shoulder-width apart.
- Weight is on the balls of the feet at all times to maintain balance.
- Knees are slightly flexed.
- Hands are held in close proximity to the rear shoulder.
- A greater amount of weight is distributed to the back leg.
- Both eyes are facing the pitcher.
- A soft, controlled movement is used so the swing is not starting from a dead standstill.

The recommended stance is a **square stance**: the feet are perfectly aligned, each equidistant from home plate. A hitter should be able to draw an imaginary straight line that extends from the toes of his back foot to the front foot and then directly out to the pitcher. An **open stance** is when the front foot is positioned farther from home plate. A **closed stance** is when the front foot is positioned closer to home plate.

All three of these stances are used and used successfully. What is important is that regardless of where a hitter's front foot starts, it should land in the square position. This enables him to drive inside, middle, and outside strikes. This is why a square stance is suggested. It keeps things simple.

Hitters get into trouble when they start open in their stance and then land open with their stride. They struggle with outside strikes and also lose a degree of power because their hips are slightly open before the swing. Less torque, less power. Hitters standing in a closed stance who stride closed have difficulty handling inside strikes. Their hips are blocked off, which forces their swing to travel around their body at a reduced speed.

Hitters can land *slightly* open or *slightly* closed and still achieve full plate coverage; it just shouldn't be drastic. Starting and finishing

A square stance keeps things simple in terms of balance and stride direction.

How Far from the Plate?

Most hitters stand deep in the batter's box to give themselves a longer look at each incoming pitch. This gives them the most time to determine whether they'll swing or take the pitch. This is especially important when facing a hard thrower. Hitters may opt to move up in the box against a soft thrower or a pitcher who throws a lot of off-speed pitches. It speeds things up when facing a soft thrower, and against a breaking ball pitcher, the hitter can attack the pitch just as it breaks instead of during its maximum break.

How close to stand to the plate or how far from it depends on the hitter. First, the batter must make certain he achieves full plate coverage. To check, take three slow-motion swings and stop at the point of contact. The first is on a pitch down the middle; the second, an inside strike; and the third, an outside strike. Make sure the hips are rotated when doing this. If you're covering each region with the barrel of the bat, your position is good.

A hitter who has greater success with pitches middle-in should position himself closer to the plate as opposed to being off the plate near the back of the box.

Lastly, consider your strengths. Hitters who like inside strikes generally stand a little closer to the plate. This pulls the strike zone in toward them, so the strike zone better matches their hitting zone. Hitters who like pitches out over the plate stand a bit farther off the plate. This pushes the strike zone away from them. Factor in your strengths when taking your stance in the box.

square simply provides the hitter with the best chance of delivering the barrel in balance with maximum force to all pitch locations.

Stride

The stride is a short, controlled step with the front foot that travels approximately three to six inches in length. It gets the swing going, allowing the hitter to start his body moving so he's not swinging from a standstill. Without the stride, hitters often fall back to their heels and drop their rear shoulder in an attempt to generate power. They hit flat-footed. Hitters will also typically drift out to their front leg and hit off their front foot when opting against the use of a stride.

To swing the bat at maximum force and to cover the entire strike zone, the batter must properly execute the stride. It's a preswing movement that places the batter in his optimum hitting position.

STRIDE DIRECTION. The stride should always land in the square position so that the hitter will achieve balance and full plate coverage. This places him in an excellent position to attack the ball. Stride direction is rarely discussed when it is performed correctly but is discussed when it veers off course.

Stepping open (or stepping in the bucket) makes the hitter vulnerable to pitches on the outside part of the plate. Even if the hitter is able to make contact with an outside pitch, the swing will lack authority. The lower body will be moving away from the pitch location, and the upper body will be fighting to stay over home plate. Good hitters have the upper and lower body working in tandem, not fighting each other.

A hitter who strides closed is able to handle pitches on the outer half of the plate but struggles with inside strikes. The hips are blocked and are unable to fully rotate. This diminishes bat speed and disrupts a hitter's path to the ball. Because his hips cannot clear, his hands (and bat) must travel around his hips and take a longer path to the ball. This results in getting jammed and/or hooking balls to the pull-side of the field.

STRIDE POSITION. The stride foot lands on the ball (or front part) of the foot. This keeps the weight loaded back and the head (and eyes) still. Upon landing, the foot remains in the closed position, keeping the hips closed. When the hitter decides to swing, he begins by forcefully rotating his hips. As this occurs, the front foot opens slightly and continues to turn open throughout the swing. At the completion of the swing, the stride foot is pointed to the 1:00 or 2:00 position for a right-handed hitter and the 10:00 or 11:00 position for a left-handed hitter. How much the front foot has opened depends on the location of the pitch.

The stride foot should not be open when it lands. This opens the hips prematurely and sacrifices power. Also, the front foot should not be in the closed position upon the completion of the swing. That means the hips are not rotating.

Loading

To strike the ball with maximum authority, the hitter must move his hands back first before moving them forward. This is called

The stride is a small step that lands on the ball of the foot and toward the pitcher. Notice how the hitter's weight remains balanced on his rear leg.

loading. As the stride foot travels forward, the hands move back to the launching position. This action is often referred to as separation: the foot and hands move in opposite directions.

Loading the hands is essential, but it's a small movement. The hands simply push straight back approximately three to five inches to the launch position before delivering the forward swing. The launch position is somewhere around shoulder height and just outside the rear shoulder.

Where a hitter holds his hands in the stance position is not important. Where they get to before the swing is significant. Derek Jeter, for example, holds his hands well above his rear shoulder in his stance. But as the pitcher is about to deliver the ball, he gently lowers his hands before pushing them back to the launch position. As long as the hitter can comfortably get to the launch position in time and do so with consistency, his hand position in the stance is irrelevant. If he is inconsistent in getting there, he must simplify his stance.

Listed here are some common mistakes hitters make during the loading stage of the preswing and the problems they will cause:

- **No load.** The hitter swings from a dead standstill and fails to generate maximum power. He will be able to make consistent contact, but he won't drive the ball.
- **Wrapping.** This is the most common loading mistake that hitters make. The barrel of the bat wraps behind the head during the load. This is caused by the hands cocking upward and toward the ear. By doing this, the hitter creates a longer distance for the barrel to get to the point of contact. He will be late on fastballs and especially have difficulty handling inside strikes.
- **Dropping the hands (hitching).** The hands drop down in an attempt to gain more power. This can make the hitter late because of the increased movement in the preswing. It will also make the hitter susceptible to pitches up in the strike zone. Some major league hitters (for example, Barry Bonds) have a hitch in their preswing, but if you watch, they hitch very early, which gives them time to raise their hands back up to the launch position.

- **Pulling the hands inward.** Pulling the hands in toward the body during the load restricts the swing. Hitters who are too conservative and just look to make contact frequently do this. The hitter will be able to handle pitches out over the plate but be forced to execute an inside-out swing on pitches middle-in. An inside-out swing means the lead arm (bottom hand) dominates and the barrel drags behind. Pitches that should be turned on and driven will be pushed to the opposite field.

Of the five tools, I think the hardest to find is a pure hitter; therefore, it is the most coveted. I think the biggest factor is soundness of his approach. Does his hitting approach allow him to stay back and read the pitch? Or does he have to commit early to his swing? Players who swing and miss will have difficulty hitting for high average.

—Steve Smith, head baseball coach, Baylor University

Hip Rotation

The rotation of the hips provides two primary benefits to the swing. First, it speeds up the bat and engages the lower half of the body (legs, lower back, abdominal muscles). This gives the hitter more bat speed and power. Second, it clears a path for the hands to take a direct route to the ball. The opportunity for the hitter to deliver a short, punishing swing enables him to see the ball a little longer before committing his hands to the swing.

The action of hip rotation is led by the front hip. Coaches often tell hitters to pivot on their back foot, which is a good thought, but it's actually the lead hip that generates the torque. The rear foot pivoting is a result of the hips firing. That being said, if telling the hitter to pivot is what gets him to explosively rotate his hips, then it's good advice.

When a hitter swings the bat, the hips and hands actually start simultaneously. But because the hands start farther back from the hips, the hips lead the hands in the swing. This is important because it clears a path for the hands and allows the lower body to help generate bat speed. Hitters sometimes get their hands in front of their hips in the sequence of their swing. They may look good at the finish, but in reality, they swung the bat with only the upper half of their body.

The degree of hip rotation depends on the location of the pitch. On inside strikes, there is maximum hip rotation. The point of contact is farther in front, so the hips must clear rapidly and forcefully to get the barrel of the bat out. The midsection should be facing slightly to the pull-side of the pitcher at the completion of the swing on inside strikes. Outside strikes require minimal hip rotation. Because the point of contact is farther back, the rotation must be controlled. If the hips fire open completely, it will pull the upper body away from the pitch and cause the barrel to drag.

STIFF FRONT LEG. In order for a hitter to forcefully rotate the hips, the front leg must stiffen. The stride foot lands soft, but the front leg must

This is the start of a great swing. The hips begin to rotate as the hands pull forward and down. The barrel of the bat remains above the ball, until it eventually levels off at contact.

then firm up to fire the hips. A bent front leg is devastating to hip rotation. A hitter's weight leaks out to his front foot as he swings, slowing hip rotation dramatically. The front leg must act as a brace to control weight shift and keep the hitter's body behind the ball at contact.

A bent front leg also brings the head forward. When the eyes move forward, it's more difficult to track the incoming pitch. Determining whether the pitch is a ball or strike, a fastball or breaking ball, becomes much more challenging. In addition, every pitch looks faster than it's actually traveling. Anytime the eyes move toward an object that's moving toward it, the object appears to be traveling faster. This causes the hitter to tense up and hurry his swing, as opposed to staying back, relaxing, and reacting to a good pitch.

Swing Path

The path of the swing dictates how consistent a hitter is in striking the ball hard. An uppercut can produce balls that are driven deep, but it will also generate a lot of pop flies, foul balls, swings and misses, and topped ground balls. A swing that descends through the strike zone can result in driven balls that carry, but it will produce a lot of hard ground balls, foul balls, and balls that are clipped at the bottom and popped up in the air. A level swing provides the hitter with the broadest hitting surface for the longest period of time through the hitting zone. A level swing produces the most hard-hit balls.

Because the hands begin above the strike zone, the forward swing starts on a descending path to the ball. This gives the hitter leverage (power) and keeps the barrel above the ball. The bottom hand begins to pull the knob of the bat toward the ball. As the hips turn, the hands begin to flatten out and the bat starts to level off as it enters the hitting zone. The top hand then takes over the swing, unhinges, and delivers the barrel of the bat to the ball.

POINT OF CONTACT. When the barrel meets the ball, the hands are in the palm-up, palm-down position. The top-hand palm faces the sky, and the bottom-hand palm faces the ground. The arms should not be at extension at the point of contact. They should be near extension, but not fully extended. The hitter needs to explode through the ball, and he loses that explosion power if he has reached full extension before contacting the ball. The hitter gets to extension with his swing shortly after he has struck the ball.

The swing remains level through contact and continues on that path after the ball has left the bat. This is the difference between merely hitting the ball and driving the ball. When the batter hits through the ball and keeps his swing on path, he drives it with power.

Following are some checkpoints to look for in a good swing at the point of contact:

- Front leg is stiff.
- Hips are rotated.
- Rear foot is pivoted.
- Rear leg is in L-shape.
- Hands are in the palm-up, palm-down position.
- Arms are near full extension.
- Head is down, looking just in front of the point of contact.

A good, balanced position at the point of contact consists of a stiff front leg, hips rotated along with pivot foot, hands in palm-up, palm-down position, and eyes locked down on the baseball. Notice how the body stays behind the ball at contact.

*Balance, hand speed, and a good swing path are important ele-
ments to being a good hitter. I also look for guys who have a knack
for squaring the ball up [barrel to the middle of the baseball]. You
can be more forgiving with a player's swing mechanics if he seems
to be able to consistently square the ball up. Some hitters just have
a great feel.*

—Chris Pittaro, director of pro scouting, Oakland Athletics

Weight Shift

In a batting stance, there is more weight carried on the back leg
than on the front. The front foot takes the stride to start the swing,
and the back foot remains anchored to fire the hips and engage the
lower body.

When the hitter swings, there is a transfer of weight from the
back leg to the baseball. There is a controlled weight shift behind
the barrel of the bat to supply the swing with maximum energy. If
the hitter keeps his weight on his back leg throughout the swing, he
is not getting everything through the ball.

Once the bat flattens out, the hitter delivers
the barrel on a level path, which provides the
greatest chance of square contact.

Some hitters have a more pronounced weight shift. Others employ a weight shift that is barely noticeable. This depends on their style of hitting and their strengths. But there must be some degree of weight shift with every hitter.

A point for hitters to be wary of is shifting the weight prematurely. A hitter's weight should not shift forward in front of his swing. It should not come forward with the stride foot or move forward with the upper body toward the incoming pitch. It comes slightly behind the swing.

Finish

The finish (or follow-through) completes the swing. A hitter who fails to complete his swing is often guilty of decelerating his bat speed prematurely. This commonly occurs when a hitter is timid and only *hopes* to make contact. He is careful with his swing. The follow-through should be strong to ensure bat speed is maintained through contact.

The bat remains on a level path after contact to make sure the barrel does not ascend out of the zone prematurely and clip the top of the ball on its way out.

There is no specific position in which a hitter must finish his swing. It should be somewhere slightly above shoulder height. If the swing finishes dramatically high, the hitter risks ascending out of his swing path prematurely. If it's too low, he risks cutting his swing off and rolling his top hand too early.

After contact, the top hand turns over and the arms break at the elbows. The hands then ascend upward and fold over above the shoulder. Hitters should think about finishing with their hands, not their whole upper body. Breaking at the elbows minimizes shoulder movement and enables the head to stay down through contact. This helps maintain balance and keeps the swing through the hitting zone as long as possible. When the arms and shoulders rise up in the follow-through, the hitter pulls up and falls back to his heels. This type of finish is indicative of a swing that pulls up and out of the strike zone too quickly, resulting in swings and misses as well as topped ground balls.

This completes a brief overview of swing mechanics. Good hitters understand the fundamentals, so when there is a breakdown, they can go to the drawing board and pinpoint the problem.

Hitting Pitch Locations

Ask 100 kids where they like their pitches, and 99 of them will respond, "Right down the middle." Unfortunately, the pitcher on the mound is taught to avoid throwing pitches down the middle whenever possible. As pitchers progress, they become more efficient at throwing their pitches to specific areas of the strike zone. They target the perimeters of the horizontal and vertical strike zone to get hitters out.

To maintain a high batting average, hitters must be proficient at hitting pitches in all parts of the strike zone. If they're able to handle inside, outside, high, and low strikes, the pitcher will have a difficult time recording an out.

Inside Strikes

There are two integral factors to turning on and driving an inside strike: starting the swing sooner and full rotation of the hips. The

Switch-Hitting: Great in Theory, but Difficult in Reality

Some of the greatest offensive players from the past and present were switch-hitters. Mickey Mantle, Pete Rose, Eddie Murray, Chipper Jones, and Carlos Beltran are just a few examples. On the flip side, many more great hitters have done their damage from just one side of the plate: Babe Ruth, Ted Williams, Frank Robinson, George Brett, and Albert Pujols.

Switch-hitting does offer some benefits, but the positives have to outweigh the negatives for a hitter to make the commitment to hitting from both sides of the plate. There is merit to the fact that breaking pitches that break in toward the hitter's hands are easier to hit than those that break away from them, especially when the hitter is fooled on the pitch. The hitter also has a little more time to see the ball when it's thrown from an opposite-armed pitcher. But those points are not enough to take on the project of switch-hitting.

First, there are certain individuals who possess the muscle coordination to effectively swing the bat from both sides of the plate. They have an innate ability, while others don't, no matter how hard they work. If the swing from the opposite side lacks quickness, fluidity, strength, and balance, it's not worth moving forward.

Second, most hitters who make the switch swing naturally from the left side and add the right side (one example is Chipper Jones). Because most pitchers are right-handed, the majority of the typical (left-handed) switch-hitter's at-bats will be taken from his natural side. For a natural right-handed hitter to learn to hit left-handed, it had better be because he possesses blazing foot speed. The right-handed hitter has to realize that the majority of his at-bats (about 75 percent of the time) will be from his unnatural, less-experienced side of the plate.

Hitters who are natural right-handers and decide to hit from both sides are generally mediocre hitters who are fleet-footed. Willie McGee is a perfect example. McGee was a light-hitting outfielder who ran very well. In order for him to have a shot in the major leagues, speed was going to be his ticket, and the left-

continued

Becoming an effective switch-hitter entails innate talent and a strong work ethic.

handed hitter's batter's box is a little closer to first base. He spent his off-seasons taking 500 left-handed swings a day to develop.

Players who possess the ability to hit from both sides have to make a decision to commit to switch-hitting if they're serious about it. It can't just be something they fool around with and try in a game when the score is lopsided. If they decide to switch-hit, they must increase their practice time and take twice as many swings from their unnatural side. They must learn to train their eyes to learn the strike zone from the opposite side and, through trial and error, begin to understand their strengths, weaknesses, hitting zone, common faults, and so on. This takes time and practice.

Lastly, once the hitter decides to take the plunge and switch-hit full-time, he has to understand that his statistics are going to suffer in the early stages. There will be growing pains, and the hitter must keep in mind that this is a project for his betterment in the long term. Opposing pitchers will attack the hitter just as hard regardless of which side of the plate he's standing, so there is going to be some failure from the opposite side.

There are great benefits to switch-hitting, and it makes absolute sense in theory. But the reality is that it takes certain physical and emotional skills, not to mention a resilient work ethic, to pull it off.

combination of these two ingredients gets the barrel of the bat out front to strike the ball. Contact must be made out in front of home plate on an inside strike. If the ball travels too deep, the hitter will get jammed (hitting the ball below the barrel), or he'll freeze and take the pitch.

When the eyes recognize that the pitch is inside, the reaction must be immediate. The hips and hands must get going right away. Because the pitch is closer to the body, hitters often get defensive. This cannot happen. On an inside strike, the hitter must go on the attack. He must take the action to the pitch and fire the hips and hands. The top hand must be active early to get the barrel out as well. Once contact is made, the hitter remains in the palm-up, palm-down position as long as possible.

If the hips fail to rotate, the swing is forced to travel around the body. An elongated swing will not suffice on an inside strike. The barrel won't get to the point of contact in time, and the hitter will get jammed.

The swing starts sooner on an inside strike so the barrel can meet the ball out in front of the plate. Explosive hip rotation is critical to turning on inside strikes.

EXPOSING THE HITTER. Pitchers look to expose weaknesses in the hitter. A pitcher may attack the inside part of the plate if the hitter he's facing

- Has a long swing or casts out and swings with his arms
- Fails to rotate his hips
- Employs a closed stance
- Dives in toward home plate with his stride
- Lunges forward with his stride, getting his weight out on his front foot

A hitter who is guilty of any these signs may be served a steady diet of inside fastballs.

Outside Strikes

The outside strike is driven to the opposite field. But how? This is a skill that is easier said than done and plagues a lot of aggressive hitters.

The primary factor is to see the ball longer. Let the ball travel deeper into the hitting zone so the point of contact is just off the rear hip. The top hand keeps the barrel of the bat up, and hip rotation is minimized to enable the upper body to stay over and through the ball.

Many hitters see that the ball is outside, know to hit it to the opposite field, but fail to let the ball get deep. If contact is made out front, it's nearly impossible to drive the ball the other way. The hitter typically will hit a rollover ground ball to the pull-side of the infield or will decelerate his swing, causing the barrel to drag and loft a lazy fly ball to the opposite field. The force of the swing is delivered farther back in the strike zone. A hitter must be patient and let the ball travel longer.

On middle and inside strikes, the role of the top hand is to get the barrel out. On outside strikes, the top hand needs to stay strong to keep the barrel up. The common mistake a hitter makes on outside pitches is he lets the top hand drag in an attempt to get the barrel level and push the ball to the opposite field. This often results in the barrel dipping beneath the ball and producing fly balls, pop-ups, and foul balls. The top hand must keep the barrel up and deliver it with force to the middle of the baseball. The hitter should think about hammering down through the ball when letting the pitch travel deeper in the zone.

EXPOSING THE HITTER. A pitcher may attack the outside part of the plate if the hitter he's facing

- Employs an open stance
- Steps open or steps in the bucket
- Pulls off the ball with his front shoulder or looks like he's trying to pull everything
- Gives off body language that he's very anxious

High Strikes

Pitches up in the strike zone are inviting. The ball is closer to the eyes and looks bigger than a pitch lower in the strike zone. On high strikes, the hitter raises his hands and levels off on the pitch. He

The key to driving an outside strike is striking the ball deeper in the hitting zone.

must be disciplined to stay through the ball palm-up, palm-down to drive this pitch with power. When the eyes see that the pitch is up, the hitter must think to get his hands up.

A high strike out over the plate is easier to drive because the hitter has more time to get his hands up. Because outside strikes are struck later in the hitting zone, it affords the hitter more time to level off on high strikes. A high strike on the inside part of the plate is more difficult to handle. The hitter needs to raise his hands up and get the barrel out very quickly. Often, the barrel doesn't get to the ball in time, and the hitter gets jammed and pops the pitch up. This is why pitchers use high and inside fastballs as an "out" pitch. The location is tough to get to for the hitter.

The most common mistake on high strikes is that the batter attempts to swing up at the pitch. The bat is pulled up and the barrel drags behind. This produces a lot of pop-ups, foul balls, and swings and misses. Another frequent mistake is that the hitter raises his barrel up with his top hand only. He attempts to get his barrel up to the ball by turning his wrist over, but this type of swing generally produces a topspin ground ball.

EXPOSING THE HITTER. A pitcher may throw high strikes if the hitter he's facing

- Has a wide stance
- Holds his hands low in the stance
- Has a hitch (drops his hands) in his preswing
- Lacks plate discipline

Low Strikes

To hit for a high average, hitters must become proficient at handling low strikes. Pitchers target the lower region of the strike zone because it's farther from the hitter's eyes and low strikes generally produce ground balls. Knowing that pitchers are typically coached to throw the ball down, hitters need to practice hitting these pitches.

To drive a low strike, the batter must go down with his back leg as he rotates. This lowers his body to the ball and enables him to swing the bat on a level (or near level) path on the incoming pitch. Swinging the bat on a level path gives the hitter the best chance of solid contact, and by going down with the rear leg, the batter is engaging the lower half of the body. He's delivering the barrel with his hands, wrists, hips, lower back, abdominal muscles, and legs.

The upper body remains the same. It's the lower body that does all the work on low strikes. The hitter must train himself to think "legs" when his eyes recognize that the pitch is down in the strike zone.

A common error is to simply drop the barrel down to the ball on a low strike. From time to time, the hitter will catch the ball square and hit it hard. But more often than not, he'll swing through it, pop it up, foul it off, or catch it off the end of the bat. When the bat is angled down, there is little margin for error and it reduces the chances of solid contact. Another path hitters travel to hit low strikes is bending the front knee and going down to the ball with their upper body. From this position, the hitter will likely pound a ground ball down into the ground.

EXPOSING THE HITTER. A pitcher may throw low strikes if the hitter he's facing

- Has a rigid stance with no flex in the knees
- Holds his hands high in the stance
- Has an aggressive stride that carries the weight out onto the front foot
- Has a swing path that descends through the strike zone

Hitting Breaking Balls

Just when hitters are confident with their swing and timing and with different pitch locations, pitchers throw another wrinkle into the mix: they learn to throw and command breaking pitches. Breaking balls add two elements into the hitting equation. They're slower, which can disrupt the hitter's timing, and they move—laterally and downward.

For hitters facing breaking pitches at the middle school or high school level, a good piece of advice is to simply lay off of them. Pitchers with minimal experience throwing breaking pitches have difficulty commanding them. Most of the strikes they get throwing breaking balls are from swings and misses. Hitters are lured into swinging at slower pitches and often chase them out of the strike zone. It's uncommon to see a pitcher get called strike after called strike with his breaking pitch, so hitters can circumvent breaking balls by simply waiting the pitcher out. Let the breaking pitch out of the strike zone be called for a ball and then attack the forthcoming fastball. Think about it. What would you rather hit?

At higher levels, pitchers gain better control of their arsenal of pitches and force hitters to learn to hit breaking balls. It doesn't necessarily mean a hitter has to swing at every breaking ball thrown for a strike. With less than two strikes in the count, the hitter can remain stubborn and wait for a fastball. But with two strikes or when facing a pitcher with excellent command of his breaking ball, the hitter has to hit the breaking pitch.

Pitch Recognition

The first step to hitting a breaking pitch is recognition. A hitter needs to determine as quickly as possible that the incoming pitch is not a fastball. Sometimes a hitter can pick this up in the pitcher's delivery. Perhaps the pitcher slows down or speeds up the pace of his pitching motion. This should alert the hitter that something other than a fastball is coming. Some pitchers change their release point when throwing a breaking pitch. If the release point is higher or lower than the arm slot of his fastball, the hitter should be aware that a breaking pitch is on its way. Pitchers may also have a tendency to "wrap" their throwing hand prematurely. In other words, as they bring their arm to the point of release, their hand is turned inward to impart spin on the ball.

These are just a few examples of how pitchers may tip their pitches. At times, a hitter may read that a breaking pitch is coming but won't be able to articulate exactly what tipped him off. That's OK; things happen quickly, and if he merely senses something different in the delivery, he's less likely to get fooled.

More polished pitchers don't tip their pitches. Everything about their delivery remains the same. This makes pitch recognition more difficult for the hitter. He needs to focus on the release point and pick up the rotation on the ball as early as possible. A fastball has backward rotation (backspin) and shoots down out of the pitcher's hand. A breaking pitch has spin that tumbles forward (overhand curveball) or tilts slightly sideways (slider). When the hitter is able to distinguish that the pitch does not have backward rotation but rather forward or sideways rotation, he needs to keep his hands back and track the pitch for a longer period of time.

The more breaking pitches a hitter sees, the better he'll become at pitch recognition. It's a skill that takes time. Extra batting practice is a good time to work on pitch recognition. Have a pitcher throw from a reduced distance and mix up throwing fastballs and spinning breaking balls. It doesn't even have to be a good breaking pitch. The point is for the hitter to practice recognizing balls that come out of the pitcher's hand differently.

Hitting the Breaking Pitch

Once the hitter has recognized a breaking pitch is on its way, two components are essential to striking the pitch with force: (1) The hitter must do his best to keep his weight back but—equally important—also keep his hands back. If the hitter gets out on his front foot and carries his hands forward, he's resigned himself to a very weak swing. If he glides forward, but keeps his hands back, he's got a chance to drive the ball. (2) The hitter must deliver the barrel to where the ball is going to be, not where he originally sees it. So many breaking balls are topped or swung over because the hitter fires his hands to where his eyes pick up the pitch. That's what hitters have been doing since they first wielded a bat. But as a breaking ball travels, it will break laterally and downward. (How much lateral and downward break depends on the release point.) The hitter must factor in the break and deliver his barrel to where the ball will be as it enters the hitting zone. This is critical to striking the ball square.

A big mistake hitters make is trying to pull breaking pitches. This inevitably gets the hitter's weight or hands out too early. They must track the ball long and think about hitting the ball to the middle or opposite field. This will keep their front shoulder in and enable them (and their swing) to stay on the ball longer. This doesn't mean a breaking ball can't be hit hard to the pull-side, but the hitter should refrain from thinking "pull" because his timing will suffer (from being too early).

Lastly, hitters often give breaking balls too much credit. If a hitter thinks he can't hit a breaking pitch, he won't hit a breaking pitch. Hitters should take an educated approach to the plate with them to maintain their level of confidence. Know how and how much the pitch breaks, if the pitcher is throwing it for strikes, and when he's throwing it. Pay attention to his pitch patterns. When a hitter digs his feet in the batter's box armed with information, he gives himself a much better chance of succeeding.

The Strike Zone Versus the Hitting Zone

The definition of *strike zone* is "that space over home plate that is between the batter's armpits and the top of the knees when the batter assumes his natural stance." Hitters come in all different shapes and sizes, so the vertical strike zone does change with each hitter. In addition, umpires have their personal interpretation of the strike zone. It's important that hitters are attentive to the umpire's strike zone for that particular day. A hitter can stick with his own interpretation during his at-bat—that is, until he gets to two strikes. Then he must shift his opinion to that of the man behind the mask.

The *hitting zone* is defined by each individual hitter. Simply stated, a batter's hitting zone represents the areas within the strike zone where he experiences consistent success. Some like the ball down in the strike zone, while others like pitches up in the strike zone. A pitch on the inside part of the plate is favorable to some, while others like the ball out over the plate.

Note that there have been bad-ball hitters whose hitting zone extended outside of the strike zone: Hall of Famers Yogi Berra, Dave Winfield, and Kirby Puckett and All-Star Vladimir Guerrero, to name a few.

Consider that the term is *batting average*—a collective average of the total number of at-bats. Hitters go through periods when they perform above their average and experience stages when they perform below their average. Performance within the strike zone also contributes to batting average and how a hitter approaches his at-bats. Major league hitting charts are usually broken up in the

A good swing follows a short, direct path to the ball and stays long through it after contact. Short to it, and long through it.

nine areas of the strike zone. Hitters may have a .378 batting average when hitting pitches in one region and a .215 batting average in another. A key component to hitting for a high average is to swing at more pitches in those "hot zones."

.235	.294	.276
.378	.390	.252
.324	.334	.215

The best hitters are constantly working on expanding their hitting zone. The more they can spread out the hot zones, the greater success they'll experience and the tougher out they'll become. Hitters should assess their "cold regions" and target those areas in practice to enhance their hitting prowess.

Understanding the areas of your hitting zone is important during competition. Hitters can apply this information to a hitting plan that will have a positive impact on their results. The more pitches they swing at in their hitting zone, the better they'll do. A hitter may decide he will only swing at a pitch in a very specific zone when there are no strikes in the count. This zone may be two baseballs high by two baseballs wide. It's where a hitter would describe the pitch as being his pitch. Typically, that is somewhere in the middle of home plate.

If the hitter gets a strike on him in the count, he may expand that zone to three baseballs high by three baseballs wide. It's when the hitter gets to two strikes that he must shift his focus from his hitting zone to the strike zone. But it's not his strike zone; it's the umpire's strike zone. The worst ending to an at-bat is to be called out on strikes. The hitter has no chance of a positive result with the bat resting on his shoulder.

This is simply one sample of developing a hitting approach based on the hitting zone. It is by no means the rule. Hitters may use this approach or one that is similar to it and have success. After a period of time, that success may dwindle, and the hitter finds that he's perhaps taking too many pitches. At that point it may be time to adjust the approach.

All hitters should be familiar with their hitting zone. The objective in games is to attack as many good pitches as possible. If the pitch is outside the hitting zone and the hitter is up at the plate just hacking away, he's making a pitcher's job very easy.

A Tough Out at All Times

The final element that is evident in players who hit for high average is a never-say-die attitude. They are a tough out. They have a competitive streak that breathes fire and will never allow them to surrender to the pitcher. Great hitters battle it out each at-bat, especially when they're struggling with their timing, swing mechanics, or plate discipline.

Every time a batter steps up to the plate, he must be convinced that he is going to hit the ball hard and reach base safely. He must be convinced that there is no way this pitcher is going to get him out. He must view himself as a danger and think that the pitcher is endangered and is about to be victimized. This is not being over-confident or cocky. It's about a batter using positive thought and visualization to help his mind and body execute at their optimum levels. The pitcher deserves respect, but during this one-on-one confrontation, he will lose. Any thoughts of doubt, fear, angst, or nervousness on the part of the batter must be eliminated. Every at-bat is an opportunity for the hitter to do something great.

Is it realistic to say that a player will hit the ball hard and reach base every time up? No, it's not realistic. But it *is* realistic for a player to say to himself, "For this at-bat, right now, I will prevail." The preceding at-bats or future at-bats mean nothing. When the feet dig into the batter's box, it is the only at-bat that matters. Going 100-for-100 at the plate is virtually impossible. But going 1-for-1 not only is possible but, in the hitter's mind, is a certainty.

Even when the mechanics of the swing break down, good hitters find a way to keep their hands back and strike the ball solid.

Hitting with Two Strikes

The pitches leading up to two strikes in the count are a game of cat and mouse. The pitcher is attempting to expose a weakness in the hitter or lure him into swinging at a pitch. The hitter is looking to attack a pitch that he likes. Often, a mistake is made by the pitcher or hitter before the count gets to two strikes. But when the count gets to two strikes, the real fun begins.

Good hitters raise their level of concentration with two strikes. Weak hitters allow emotions and negative thoughts to intrude and are victimized by themselves as much as by the pitcher. A good hitter has to take on a stubborn, relentless attitude with two strikes. Their mind-set should be that of "There is no way this guy is going to get me out."

A common two-strike approach is to look for a fastball away. This guides the hitter toward seeing the pitch a little longer. With this approach, the hitter must trust himself to react to an inside fastball or adjust to an off-speed pitch. Working off the fastball away gives the hitter good plate coverage and provides him the best chance of keeping his hands back on a changeup or breaking ball.

Looking for a pitch middle-in can cause problems. The hitter's timing will be set to committing his hands early to get the barrel out. He now becomes more vulnerable to off-speed pitches and outside strikes.

Anticipating an off-speed pitch with two strikes can also be troublesome to the batter. If he sets his timing to sit back and await an off-speed pitch, he'll never catch up to the fastball. In fact, the hitter commonly freezes and never gets the bat off his shoulder. Sitting breaking ball or changeup with two strikes is very risky business.

Lastly, good hitters maintain their bat speed with two strikes. They do not slow their swing down and attempt to flick the ball to the outfield. Contact may be made a little deeper in the hitting zone, but they still deliver the barrel with authority. They're just trying to see the ball a little longer.

"A lot of hitters change their swing when they get behind in the count," says Tony Gwynn. "When they get two strikes, they're just trying to meet the ball. . . . If I have two strikes on me, that isn't going to change anything. I've still got one more opportunity to hit the ball."

Bunting for a base hit is just another weapon to have in the offensive arsenal. It keeps the defense honest and can be put to use when the hits aren't coming so easily.

Top 10 All-Time Major League Leaders in Career Batting Average

Ty Cobb	.366
Rogers Hornsby	.358
Shoeless Joe Jackson	.352
Pete Browning	.349
Ed Delahanty	.346
Tris Speaker	.345
Billy Hamilton	.344
Ted Williams	.344
Dan Brouthers	.342
Babe Ruth	.342

3
Hitting for Power

Power. It's a word that commands attention, respect, and desire. Take any skill inside or outside of sports, and if you add power to it, you've made it better. Whether it's a power puncher, power pitcher, or powerful engine, it's a descriptive adjective that attracts admiration and fuels the imagination.

Before discussing how to develop more power as a hitter, it's important to address what power hitting is. Typically, hitting for power is associated with extra-base hits and home runs. Without question, those are viable results when hitting the ball powerfully. But doesn't ripping a sharp line drive through the middle also count for hitting with power? It's not limited to hitting the ball far. It also includes hits that leave the bat with extraordinary exit velocity speed.

Developing more power at the plate should help a hitter's power numbers along with his batting average. The more balls that leave the bat with authority, the greater the chance that a ball will find open real estate. Understanding this point is very important to players who do not consider themselves power hitters. If a player's offensive game is centered around hitting singles and getting on base, he, too, can better his craft by developing more power. Simply put, a stronger hitter is a better hitter.

Of the five tools, hitting for power is tops for me. One swing of the bat, especially with runners on base, can make a huge impact on the game.

—Richard Rembielak, head baseball coach, Wake Forest University

---

A power hitter can change the face of a game with one swing of the bat.

The Best Hitters of All Time

Ask a crowded room of baseball fans to name the best hitters of all time. The baseball historians will remain loyal to Babe Ruth, Lou Gehrig, and Joe DiMaggio. The golden age of baseball boasted the likes of Ted Williams, Mickey Mantle, Willie Mays, and Hank Aaron. Fans of the modern era will throw out names like Mike Schmidt, George Brett, Ken Griffey Jr., and Barry Bonds. It has yet to be determined how the careers of Alex Rodriguez and Albert Pujols will measure up against the greatest of all time, but they are certainly on the path to securing a spot in Cooperstown.

All of these hitters were (or are) exceptionally gifted. And all of them hit for power. They didn't just hit the ball when it entered the strike zone—they *punished* it. These men are categorized as being very dangerous when wielding a baseball bat. One mistake by the pitcher, and the baseball is headed toward a world of pain.

While these players mentioned have earned much of their acclaim via home run totals, they also hit for average. Hard ground balls and line drives afford the defensive players less reaction time to make a play. The hitting lanes for a power hitter are wider than those for a hitter with less power.

When discussing great hitters, fans also cultivate another crop of names. Ty Cobb, Pete Rose, Rod Carew, Tony Gwynn, and Wade Boggs are players who experienced phenomenal success at the plate. They are not mentioned along with Ruth or Bonds because they didn't put up big power numbers. But make no mistake; these hitters had power, and they were capable of hitting a lot more home runs. They just dispensed their power in a different way. They felt they were at their best (and most valuable) by seeing the ball longer, using the whole field, and lacing line drives for singles and doubles.

Cobb actually led the league in home runs during the dead-ball era with nine in 1909. He twice hit 12 in his career and in those years drove in more than 100 runs. Rose clubbed 160 career home runs, including 16 in 1966 and 1969, but his efforts were best spent scattering 4,256 hits over a 24-year career. Carew belted 14 round trippers and drove in 100 runs in 1977 to complement his seven AL batting titles. Boggs hit 24 in 1987 but decided that pounding balls off of the Green Monster at Fenway Park was a better way to get on base. Gwynn flirted with power hitting by knocking out 17 homers in 1997 and still managed to lead the National League in hitting at a .372 clip. But Gwynn had greater success driving base hits all over the field, as shown by his nine NL batting titles.

These players had power and used that strength to drive balls through the infield and outfield gaps. Young players who consider themselves contact hitters should not ignore the benefits of strength, nor should they neglect seeking to hit the ball with more force. It will only make them a more productive, offensive player. Ted Williams, who was the last major league player to hit .400 (when he batted .406 in 1941), believed that power and average went hand in hand. "To hit .400, you've got to have the power to keep the defense back and spread out."

Developing More Power at the Plate

The player who is seeking to develop more power at the plate must concentrate on four areas to achieve his goal. Thinking that he simply needs to hit more home runs is not going to suffice. Hitting for power entails improving strength, perfecting technique, exercising an approach for power hitting in certain counts and situations, and, lastly, attitude. These are the most significant areas for a hitter to target when attempting to improve power.

Attitude

It was mentioned last, but attitude comes first. A hitter can have flawed technique or no real approach at the plate, or he may never work on improving strength, but he might still hit with power. If he lacks attitude at the plate, however, he is not going to realize his power potential and certainly won't drive the ball with consistency.

What does it mean to have attitude when hitting? It means having a mind-set where the hitter is looking to attack the ball. He stands at the plate with an aura of confidence. His eyes are relaxed and clearly focused on the incoming pitch. He stays back (in balance) in anticipation of a good pitch to hit, and when he sees it, he explodes on the ball. He fires his hips, fires the barrel out with his hands, and transfers his weight behind the bat.

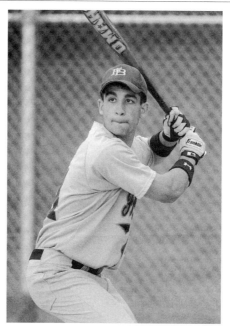

The first step to driving the ball with power is *believing* you'll drive the ball with power.

Great hitters have quiet confidence at the plate. They believe that there is nothing they can't handle. Making contact is a given and is not their ultimate goal. Their mission is to unleash a forceful swing that impacts the middle of the baseball and continues right through the back of the baseball. Strong hitters don't pull the trigger to hit the ball. They pull it to commit an act of assault.

Hitters often lament how they can improve their bat speed. Rather than tinker with technique or question bat weight and length, hitters should first explore what's happening above the shoulders. Are they committing to attacking the ball, or are they just trying to ensure contact? It is amazing how bat speed can pick up when a hitter is told to let it loose. Suddenly, the hips work faster and the bat travels through the hitting zone at a higher rate of speed. Hitters must work within the parameters of sound mechanics and balance. But every now and then, they need to be reminded that they are the offensive player. Their job is not to put the ball in play but to hit the ball hard. Attitude and bat speed are directly linked.

Simply trying to put the ball in play is not a philosophy that will produce optimum bat speed, technique, or results. Typically, players who have contact as their goal will do one of two things. They will get out on their front foot and "feel" for the ball. This displaces their weight forward, putting them in a position to swing the bat with their upper body only. The hips can't forcefully rotate once the weight shifts out to the front foot. This produces a bevy of weak ground balls or shallow fly balls.

The second path "contact" hitters travel is that they see the ball too long (to make sure of pitch type and location). They never get the barrel of the bat out and appear to fight everything off to the opposite field. Hitting the ball too deep in the hitting zone gives the hitter little time or space to generate bat speed. He survives at the plate rather than being the aggressor. Hitters should always remember that without risk, there is no major reward. They have to commit to swinging the bat early enough to give the barrel a chance of meeting the ball out front with force.

A power hitter does not have fear at the plate. He does not fear failure and does not fear the baseball.

—Chris Pittaro, director of pro scouting, Oakland Athletics

DEVELOPING AN ATTITUDE. Pitchers can fool hitters, but a hitter can't fool himself. If he doesn't have the confidence to sustain a positive attitude at the plate, he must work toward building that assertiveness from the ground up.

Strength training has an immediate physical and psychological impact. Over time, the bat feels lighter and the swing feels faster. With this in mind, hitters will have more comfort seeing the ball longer because they feel quicker. Having more time to recognize pitch types and locations will improve a hitter's barrel accuracy. Striking the ball off the barrel optimizes power.

Work in the weight room makes the body stronger. Stronger forearms, lower back, abdominals, and the like will enable a hitter to produce a swing that is more powerful. Hitters will notice their

The hitter is the hunter, not the hunted.

hits leaving the bat with more speed and distance. Suddenly, hitting becomes a little more fun. All of this builds confidence, presence at the plate, and attitude.

Tee work, soft toss, and batting practice improve technique, hand-eye coordination, strength, and quickness. These combined elements make a hitter feel more prepared at the plate. Instead of worrying about the stride, load, or swing path, the hitter can focus on getting a good pitch and executing a swing that he has practiced countless times. Hitters who feel prepared have peace of mind.

Paying attention to the opposing pitcher also improves confidence. If the hitter picks up on pitch patterns and approaches his at-bat with an educated guess of the what, when, and where of each pitch, he'll feel as if he has an edge. His attitude will be that of the hunter and not the hunted.

As mentioned, hitters can't fool themselves. They can't wake up one day and just decide to have attitude at the plate. Attitude evolves through hard work, preparation, and understanding hitting. But once a hitter's got it, he'll never want to hit without it again.

The best position players are able to hit first, and then they develop more power as they progress. It's usually not the other way around. To hit for power, players have to improve their strength and help their bodies fill out. It also entails getting better at pitch recognition, keeping leverage and balance throughout the swing, and having an approach at the plate.

—Mike Garlotti, scout, Colorado Rockies

Technique

The mechanics of the swing were discussed in Chapter 2. From a batting average standpoint, executing solid mechanics breeds consistency. From a power standpoint, perfect technique means getting the most out of the swing, getting every ounce of strength and energy to the right place at the right time. Good technique provides a foundation for the hitter to reach optimum power.

A general term that is absolutely necessary to generating power is *balance*. The hitter must be balanced throughout his swing to maximize his power. Swinging in balance maximizes quickness and explosiveness. It also keeps the head still, enabling the hitter to track the ball and deliver the barrel to the middle of the ball consistently.

"Power is typically the last thing to come for a hitter," says Chris Pittaro, director of pro scouting for the Oakland Athletics. "Players need time to mature physically, to understand their strengths and how they're being pitched to. It also takes time to understand that most of the power comes from being in balance and generating torque in the lower half of the body."

There are particular parts of swing mechanics that have greater significance in generating power. A batter should review each of these components—loading, hip rotation, weight shift, and extension through the baseball—when seeking to develop more power.

LOADING. To generate maximum power, the hands must move back before going forward. This is called loading, and it's integral to driving the ball with force. Loading up gets the hands moving so the forward swing does not start from a dead standstill. Also, moving the hands slightly back affords the hitter more time (and space) to get the barrel traveling at top speed.

Before the 1999 season, Atlanta Braves All-Star Chipper Jones struggled to hit with power as a right-handed hitter. Most of his power came from the left side. Following the advice of then-hitting coach Don Baylor, Jones increased his load when hitting right-handed. He previously had very little load and considered himself more of a contact hitter from that side of the plate. Increasing his load and being more aggressive spawned Jones's best year as he hammered a career-high 45 home runs and won the 1999 National League MVP award.

Increasing the distance of the load does mean the hitter needs to begin his load sooner. This allows him more time to get back to his launching position. The movement should be directly back away from incoming pitch. It should not be out away from the body, upward, behind the head, or a big shoulder turn inward. The hands should simply push back before firing forward.

The hands must move back before going forward to deliver the barrel with maximum force.

A batter can still hit the ball without loading but not with maximum power. With good hand-eye coordination and timing, he will be an adequate contact hitter. But to drive pitches with force, he's got to get his hands moving back before the forward swing.

HIP ROTATION. Rotating the hips while swinging the bat is essential for three primary reasons:

- **Hip rotation engages the lower half of the body.** It supplies power and energy from large muscle regions, including the calves, quadriceps, lower back, and abdominal muscles. Rather than swinging the bat with the hand, arms, and shoulders, the hitter delivers the barrel with the force of his entire body.
- **Hip rotation accelerates bat speed.** The faster the hips rotate, the faster the bat travels through the hitting zone. Improved bat speed results in increased power.
- **Hip rotation clears a path for the hands to fire directly to the ball.** A short, compact swing is much more powerful than a long, roundabout swing. Not only is a short swing stronger, but it also improves barrel accuracy. A powerful swing is only worth its weight if the ball is struck with the barrel of the bat.

If the hips do not rotate, the hands (and swing) are forced to travel around the body. When the hands get out away from the body, they possess less force.

The hips must rotate in a timely fashion. They initiate the forward swing. The hips lead the hands in the swing. This is integral. If the hands get in front of the hips, the batter is swinging the bat only with the upper half of his body. He may look good in the finish, but it's only aesthetic. Power from the lower body was not utilized.

WEIGHT SHIFT. There are two documented styles of hitting that are often discussed by hitting coaches. The rotation style of hitting was preached by Ted Williams in his book *The Science of Hitting*. In the 1980s Charlie Lau published his philosophies on weight-shift hitting in *The Art of Hitting .300*. Both styles of hitting are used with great success by major league hitters. Which style a hitter employs is largely based on his individual makeup and strengths.

The hips lead the hands in the swing. This is essential to engaging the lower half of the body.

Which style is better for power? The answer is both. In order to generate maximum power, the hitter must rotate his hips and have some degree of weight shift with his swing.

In the stance position, the batter begins with more weight on his back leg. Weight shift means transferring that weight from the rear leg into the point of contact. A hitter does not want to start with his weight back and finish with his weight back. (In golf, this is called a reverse pivot.) To get everything through the ball, he must transfer some weight with the swing.

The weight shift should occur *behind* the barrel (or swing). This often happens naturally but should be monitored. If the weight transfers in front of the swing, it's going to cause numerous problems. Premature weight shift diminishes hip speed, which in turn decreases bat speed.

The degree of weight shift may also depend on the location of the pitch. On pitches out over the plate, the hitter employs a more aggressive weight shift and less hip rotation. A higher degree of weight shift replaces the power lost by minimal hip rotation. On inside strikes, there is minimal weight shift and more hip rotation. The hips must fully (and quickly) rotate to get the barrel out in front of home plate on an inside strike.

EXTENSION THROUGH THE BASEBALL. Hitting coaches often discuss the importance of getting to extension when striking the baseball. Getting to extension means the arms are fully extended and the hands are in the palm-up, palm-down position. Players who fail to get to extension cut their swings off prematurely and sacrifice power. But hitters want to be careful as to exactly *when* they get to extension. A hitter does not want to be at extension at the point of contact. He wants to get to extension just after contact. The difference is very slight, but it has an impact on how much power is delivered to the ball.

Once the arms reach extension, they lose explosiveness. The swing begins to decelerate. The most powerful swings accelerate through the ball, through contact. A hitter wants to feel as if his swing is still accelerating as he's striking the ball. He should be *near* extension at contact and at *full* extension after the ball leaves the bat.

As mentioned, when a hitter fails to get to extension, he cuts his swing short. Typically, the top hand turns over prematurely, and the barrel begins to ascend out of the hitting zone at contact. Such swings produce a lot of topped ground balls.

You need to get the barrel out in front to drive a pitch middle-in, but you still have to let the ball travel. That takes trust from the hitter. By letting the ball get as deep as possible, the hitter is able to stay inside the ball and drive it with backspin. If the barrel gets out too early, the hitter will get around the ball and hit balls that hook or dive. You want to impart backspin on the ball for carry, not topspin.

—Scott Bradley, former major league player and head baseball coach,
Princeton University

Notice there is still a slight degree of flex in the arms. Extension is reached after (not at) contact when generating maximum force through the ball.

A Hitting Approach for Power

Without risk, there is no reward. Power hitters in the major leagues understand this and experience it on a daily basis. Go down the list of all-time home run leaders and then cross-check it with the list of all-time strikeout leaders (offensive). There are a lot of repeat customers on those lists, including Barry Bonds, Sammy Sosa, Mark McGwire, Eddie Murray, Frank Robinson, Mickey Mantle, and Harmon Killebrew. Current slugger Jim Thome is an example of a player who typically hits 40-plus home runs per year but also appears near the top of the strikeout list each season.

Reggie Jackson is considered one of the greatest power hitters of all time. During his career, he launched 563 homers, many of them coming in crucial moments. He was a first-ballot Hall of Famer and will be remembered as Mr. October for his postseason performances. Jackson also heads the list of striking out more than anyone in the history of baseball—by a long shot. He went down on strikes 2,597 times. That is 661 more times than the next hitter on the list, Willie Stargell. This is not a cut on Jackson but rather an affirmation that he took risks at the plate. He often committed to getting the barrel out to drive the ball with power. He was not afraid to swing and miss. Had he not taken that approach, his career total number of home runs would be far short of 563.

Jackson, a very bright man, often had an interesting way of looking at things, as exemplified in this comment: "If you play for ten years in the major leagues and have 7,000 at-bats and 2,000 hits, you've had a pretty fair career (.285 batting average). But you've gone 0-for-5,000."

The Mr. October statistics should not be misinterpreted to mean that all hitters should try to turn on and hit every pitch for power. The game situation, the count, the pitcher on the mound, and your role in the lineup all play a factor in whether to take that approach. However, hitters cannot be afraid to swing and miss if they want to hit with power. They cannot house fearful thoughts of being fooled. Jackson was a valued power hitter, and he understood that without some risk, there could be no major reward.

COMMITTING TO A PLAN. Entering each at-bat, the hitter should have a plan. The plan can be very broad, or it can be specific to each pitch during the at-bat. How broad or how specific primarily depends on the hitter. Is he a thinker? Or is he a player better served by not making things too complex and filling his head with too much thought? An example of a general plan would be to think, "I'm going to see some pitches and work a deep count." Another plan would be, "I'm going to be aggressive early in the count and look to get the barrel out front." Specific plans may be pitch to pitch, such as, "I'm looking for a fastball on the inside part of the plate." Perhaps with one strike, the hitter may adjust his plan and think, "I feel an off-speed pitch is coming, so I'm going to sit back and look off-speed."

The plan that is employed is not what's most significant. It's that the hitter has a plan and he *commits* to it. He eliminates all wavering thoughts and doubt and sets his mind to attacking the pitch he is anticipating. This gives the hitter a greater sense of confidence, self-assuredness, and presence at the plate. When the hitter is decisive about what he is looking for, he will be more decisive (and explosive) with his swing. He will be less likely to get in between or feel for pitches.

Formulating a plan (or approach) for power is based on selecting points during an at-bat where the hitter feels he is going to get a certain pitch in a certain location that he can exploit. If he gets that pitch, he must react aggressively by firing his hips, transferring weight, and getting the barrel to the ball. If he doesn't get this pitch, he must do his best to hold his hands up and take it.

An essential piece of information for a hitter to develop an approach for power is knowledge of his hitting zone. What areas of the strike zone does the hitter consistently hit for power? Does he favor pitches middle-in? Does he like them out over the plate? Would he rather have the pitch be up or down in the strike zone? Identifying these areas as power zones is critical in planning and executing an approach for power.

Also, is he a good fastball hitter? Is he a good breaking ball hitter? Some players are great at hitting fastballs but struggle to strike

Power hitters are aggressive, but selectively aggressive. If the pitch is outside of his power zone, the hitter must remain patient.

breaking balls solid even when they know they're coming. Other hitters are great at hitting breaking balls but have trouble catching up to hard fastballs. Hitters should distinguish which category they fall under and factor that into their approach.

Always take the game situation and your role into consideration. With a runner on second base and nobody out with the score tied late in the game, the number two hitter should *not* be looking to drive the ball into the left-center field gap. He should let the ball get deep, keep the barrel above the ball, and hit a ground ball to the right side of the infield. This allows the runner to advance to third base with one out for the number three hitter. Know your role and your responsibility on the team at all times.

An Educated Guess: Understanding Pitch Patterns. Committing to a plan is essential, but it helps when that plan is supported by research. There is a big difference between guessing what pitch is coming and having an educated guess.

Pitchers typically fall into patterns. Their sequence of pitches is generally based on their pitch repertoire, the pitch they can best throw for a strike, their overall command, and their "out" pitch. If the pattern they start out with is working, they will likely stick with that pattern. Pitchers go with what works for them and rarely deviate from their plan when they're experiencing success. If they're getting beaten up, they'll probably adjust their patterns to try something different.

Most patterns are very simple to pick up on if hitters are paying attention. Many pitchers throw first-pitch fastballs for a strike. Since the day they stepped on the mound, pitchers have heard their coaches preaching to get ahead. It's a much better position to pitch from 0-1 rather than 1-0. A fastball is the easiest pitch to command; therefore, first-pitch fastballs for strikes are common.

On the batter's end, hitting from an 0-1 count as opposed to hitting that first-pitch fastball makes the at-bat more complex. A greater number of variables immediately come into play. Will the pitcher now throw an off-speed pitch? Will he look to paint the corners of the plate? Will he target outside the strike zone and try to get the batter to chase? Suddenly, that first-pitch fastball would have been a good one to swing at.

It's an all-too-common practice for hitters to take the first pitch. Whether it's because they want to see a pitch or fear making a one-pitch out, it is often an opportunity wasted. Hitters should be able to see point of release and pitch velocity from the on-deck circle. If the hitter questions whether the fastball has movement, ask a hitter who's already faced the pitcher. That first pitch may be the best one he sees during the at-bat.

Pitchers employ other typical patterns. When they miss the strike zone with an off-speed pitch, they typically come back with a fastball. When they throw a fastball and get a late swing, they often come back with another fastball and try to throw it inside. When they throw a fastball and it's fouled straight back or pulled foul, they often follow with an off-speed pitch. Pitchers have patterns, but they're also trying to combat what the hitter is showing them. If the hitter pays attention, he has a good chance of formulating an educated guess.

Hitters' counts are when the pitcher has fallen behind: 1-0, 2-0, or 3-1. These are counts that provide a great opportunity for the hitter to look fastball and get the barrel out early. Hitters should visualize the pitch they're looking for and commit to it. Also, they must remind themselves that if they get that pitch, they must relax and employ a short, quick swing.

Pitchers will also attempt to get hitters out by changing planes and pitch locations. A hitter may see consecutive pitches thrown hard to the inside part of the plate. These pitches may be followed by something soft away. The hitter becomes conscious of starting his swing early and getting the barrel out and is then fooled by an off-speed pitch away. Conversely, a pitcher may throw a series of soft pitches outside to slow the hitter's eyes and get him leaning out over the plate. He then follows with a hard fastball inside in an attempt to jam or freeze the hitter.

At the highest levels of the game there are pitchers like Greg Maddux, Pedro Martinez, and Curt Schilling who are a triple threat. They have exceptional stuff, great command, and game smarts. They often counter the hitter's counter thoughts. When facing a polished pitcher, look to get him early in the count. Don't overthink. Just use your instinct and commit to it. Remember, the hitter has three strikes. He can fail twice and still succeed in the at-bat.

If the hitter consistently hits high strikes for power, he needs to capitalize when the pitcher gives him a pitch up in the zone.

Game Situation

Certain game situations call for a hitter to drive the ball with power. Hitters should always look to hit the ball hard, but there are times when an extra-base hit, a deep fly to the outfield, or a home run would greatly increase a team's chances of winning.

Listed here are a few late-game situations that call for a ball driven to the outfield:

- Runner on third base, fewer than two outs
- Runner on first base, two outs, down by a run
- Runners on first and second, two outs, down by two runs
- Bases loaded, down by three runs
- Nobody on, two outs, down by a run

Strength Training

A stronger hitter is a better hitter—this is an open-and-shut case. Athletes must make sure they're focusing on the correct muscle regions, practicing proper technique, and following an intelligible program. But weight training will provide tremendous benefits to a hitter.

Developing strength obviously pays physical dividends to a player. What often goes unspoken are the psychological benefits it provides. When a person works out, he understands that he is improving himself. He begins to see and feel physical improvements, which builds internal pride. Feeling better about yourself breeds confidence, and when a hitter strides up to the plate feeling bigger and stronger, his performance will reflect that of someone with a heightened self-esteem.

In addition, weight training decreases a player's vulnerability to injury. His body is better prepared to withstand the rigors of competition and the turns, twists, and inadvertent contact that often occur. Improved muscle endurance enables the player to stay balanced and perform at a high level from the first pitch to the last out.

A question that typically enters the equation of strength training is at what age it is recommended that a ballplayer should begin. There is no perfect answer because young adults develop at different stages of life. Ages can range from 12 to 14 years of age for beginners. The best suggestion is to seek the advice of a certified physician or trainer.

A player must pursue weight training with an understanding that he is seeking to improve strength as a baseball player. His efforts are not to be confused with working out to look good at the beach. In addition, a football player or wrestler may have an exceptional weight training program, but they are specific to those sports. A baseball player must train his body to enhance performance within the sport of baseball.

Enhancing power can be helped with strengthening of the hands and arms. A player who isn't tall or who weighs a lot can generate more bat speed by having a stronger upper body.

—Richard Rembielak, head baseball coach, Wake Forest University

A coach or certified trainer can help provide guidance in the weight room.

Plyometric, speed, and agility training are also vital to improving a player's strength, quickness, and explosiveness. Those types of training exercises will be addressed in Chapter 6.

Strength Training Programs

Much like there are numerous batting stances and styles that are workable, there are many strength training programs that are suitable and effective for ballplayers. In general, a strength training program should be productive, comprehensive, practical, and safe.

When selecting a specific program, there are many variables that factor into the equation, such as experience (beginner or advanced), the time of year (off-season, preseason, in season), the primary objective (build or maintain strength, rehabilitation), time available, and access to equipment. As already pointed out, there is more than one way to skin a cat. It's not imperative that a player uses a specific program, but it is essential that he has a quality program and that he commits to it.

The types of programs are endless. There is multiple-set training, in which the athlete performs several sets (three to five) of the same exercise at a lower weight before moving on to the next exercise. (A set represents series of repetitions in a specific exercise. For example, 10 dumbbell curls would be one set.) There is circuit training, where

A workout partner (and spotter) is helpful for motivation and assistance during training.

the athlete completes one set of an exercise and then moves on to another exercise. After he's completed a circuit (six to ten exercises), he goes through the circuit a second and third time. There is pyramid training, where the athlete performs several sets of the same exercise, but each set increases in weight and lowers in number of repetitions. There is four-day split training, where the athlete performs a number of core lift exercises and then augments his training with auxiliary exercises. Core lift exercises are bench press, squats, dead lifts, leg press, and power cleans. Auxiliary exercises would be dumbbell curls, tricep pull-downs, and upright rows.

How an athlete designs his program as to what muscle regions to work on is also optional. Some programs have the player work on his upper body for one workout session and his lower body for the following session. An athlete may also divide it up so he focuses, for example, on his chest and triceps for one session, back and biceps for the next session, and shoulders and legs for the final session. Circuit training often has the athlete working on all the muscle regions throughout each session.

For the baseball player, a general suggestion is to begin with multiple-set training three to four days per week. From there, he should progress toward pyramid or four-day split training to advance the strength development. As the season nears and during the season, he should scale back to circuit training two to three days per week.

Before moving on to some examples of specific exercises and a strength program, here are some general guidelines that athletes should follow when working hard in the weight room:

- Consult a certified trainer or coach regarding your strength training program.
- Have a lifting partner. This helps with motivation and provides a spotter.
- Do not lift the same muscle regions on consecutive days. The muscles need time to recover. (Abs and forearms are the exception to this rule.)
- Learn the proper lifting technique (form). This accelerates the strengthening process and reduces any risk of injury.
- Be sensible when selecting the amount of weight. Your only concern is improving your personal strength. Don't worry about how much your friend or the guy across the weight room is lifting.
- Stretch before and after each workout.
- Understand that there will be soreness during the initial stages of your strength training. It's part of the building and development process.
- Remember to breathe while you're lifting.
- Push yourself. The only way to enhance strength is to work hard.

Muscle Regions of Emphasis

Baseball players should work on strengthening their entire bodies, but there are some muscle regions that are of greater importance to enhancing baseball skills. The calves, thighs, midsection, lats (back), shoulders, hands, wrists, and forearms are body parts that fuel skills like throwing, running, hitting, and fielding. These muscle regions should gain considerable attention and development during strength training for baseball.

Listed next are exercises that will train the mentioned muscle regions.

CALVES

Standing Calf Raises
Position: Stand with your shoulders under the supports of a standing calf raise machine. Position your toes on the elevated stand so that your heels are hanging off the end. Keep your back straight, and grip the handlebars with your hands.
Begin: Stand up on your toes as high as you can, pause, and then lower your heels back to the starting position.

Seated Calf Raises
Position: Sit with your knees under the supports of a leg press machine. Place the balls of your feet on the foot pad, legs near extension.
Begin: Push the foot pad forward with the balls of your feet so your toes are pointed, and then lower them back to the starting position.

THIGHS

Squats
Position: Stand upright with your feet shoulder-width apart and toes pointed straight forward at the squat machine. Rest the barbell behind your neck on your traps with your hands slightly more than shoulder-width apart. Keep your back straight, your head tilted up, and your weight on the balls of your feet.
Begin: With your back remaining straight, slowly lower the weight by bending your knees until your thighs are parallel to the floor. Then push back up to the starting position. (Do not lean back or go back on your heels during this exercise.)

Leg Extensions
Position: Sit with your back straight and against the pad of the leg-extension machine and feet hooked underneath the foot bar. Grip the handles with your hands down by your waist.
Begin: Raise the bar with your feet extended as far as possible, and then lower your legs back down to the starting position.

Leg extensions and leg presses build strength in the calf, thigh, and hamstring regions.

Leg Presses

Position: Sit with the soles of your feet pressed against the platform of the leg-press machine. Slightly bend your knees. Grip the handles on the sides.

Begin: Lower the weight down slowly until your feet are near the height of your knees. Then push the weight back up slowly to the starting position.

Lunges

Position: Stand upright with your feet together. Hold a dumbbell in each hand with your palms facing inward. Keep your head looking straight forward.

Begin: Slowly take a large step forward with one leg, bending both knees. Your back knee should nearly touch the ground. Using your extended leg, thrust yourself back to the starting position, retracing the path you came down.

MIDSECTION

Sit-Ups

Position: Lie flat on your back with your knees bent and feet flat on the floor. Hold your hands behind your head.

Begin: Lift the upper half of your body as high as you can, hold the position, and then slowly return to the starting position.

Elbow-to-Knee Sit-Ups

Position: Lie flat on your back with your knees bent and feet flat on the floor. Hold your hands behind your head.

Begin: Use your abs to raise your head forward while lifting your left foot off the floor so that your knee comes toward your head. Touch your knee with your opposite-side elbow. Hold that position, and then slowly lower yourself back to the starting position.

Developing a strong abdominal region is critical to core strength.

Leg Lifts

Position: Lie flat on your back with your legs together. Place your hands by your side with the palms facing down.

Begin: Lift your legs four to six inches off the floor and hold. The legs must remain straight. Hold this position for 30 to 45 seconds, and then slowly lower them back to the floor.

Seated Rows

Position: Sit at a row machine with your back straight and feet resting on the foot pads. Lean forward and grab the handles.

Begin: Keeping your back straight, lean backward and pull the handles in toward your stomach. Pause briefly, and then return to the starting position.

LATS

Lat Pull-Downs

Position: Sit at a lat pull-down machine. Grab each end of the bar using a forward grip. Lean back slightly, making sure your feet are flat on the floor.

Begin: Pull the bar down to the upper part of your chest, just beneath your chin. Pause for a brief moment, and then let the bar back up to its starting position at a controlled pace.

Seated rows

Pull-Ups

Position: Standing beneath the pull-up bar, grab the bar with a forward grip. Position your hands outside shoulder width, completely extend your arms, and cross your feet up off the floor.

Begin: Keeping your body stationary, pull your body up so your chin rises above the bar. Pause briefly, and then lower your body back down to the starting position.

One-Arm Dumbbell Rows

Position: Stand with your left hand and left knee resting on a flat bench. Bend at the waist to form a 90-degree angle. Hang your right arm to the side, and hold a dumbbell with your palm facing inward. Keep your back straight and head tilted back.

Begin: Lift the dumbbell up to the side of your body. As it touches, pause and then lower it back down to the starting position. After you've completed a set with the right arm, switch sides to the left arm.

SHOULDERS

Dumbbell Shoulder Presses

Position: Sit upright. Grip the dumbbells with your palms facing out at shoulder height.

Dumbbell rows

Begin: Push the dumbbells straight up until your arms are extended, and then slowly return to the starting position. The dumbbells should never drop beneath your shoulders.

Lateral Raises

Position: Stand upright with your knees slightly flexed. Hold the dumbbells down at your sides with your palms facing inward.

Begin: With your arms remaining straight, raise the dumbbells out to your sides until they reach just beyond shoulder height. Then slowly return to the starting position.

Standing Flies

Position: Stand with your knees flexed and a slight bend at the waist so your back is straight at a 45-degree angle. Hold the dumbbells in toward your midsection with your palms facing inward.

Begin: Keeping your body still and your arms bent, lift the dumbbells upward and back as far as you can. The dumbbells should reach ear height, and your elbows should be at shoulder level. Then slowly return to the starting position.

Rotator Cuff (Prone Position)

Position: Lie facedown on a flat bench, and extend one arm to the side. Bend your arm at a 90-degree angle so that your upper arm is

Standing flies

parallel to the floor and your hand is hanging with the palm facing behind you.

Begin: Using a lightweight dumbbell, rotate your forearm upward until it becomes parallel to the ground. Then slowly return to the starting position.

Rotator Cuff (Side Position)

Position: Lie on your side on a flat bench. Rest your upper arm on your chest (parallel to the floor) and bent at the elbow at a 90-degree angle so your hand is hanging.

Begin: Using a lightweight dumbbell, rotate your arm upward until it becomes parallel to the ground. Then slowly return to the starting position.

HANDS, WRISTS, FOREARMS

Wrist Rolls

Position: While standing, grip the bar with both hands, and extend your arms directly out in front of you.

Begin: Roll the bar forward in your hands. Continue until the weight gets to the top, pause, and then slowly roll the bar backward until the weight returns to the starting position.

Forearm Curls (Forward Grip)

Position: Sit at the end of a bench. Hold a barbell with a forward grip (palms facing down) with your forearms resting on your thighs.

Begin: Use your wrists to curl the bar upward and back as far as you can. Then slowly return to the starting position.

Forearm Curls (Reverse Grip)

Position: Sit at the end of a bench. Hold a barbell with a reverse grip (palms facing the ceiling) with your forearms resting on your thighs.

Begin: Use your wrists to curl the bar upward and inward as far as you can. Then slowly return to the starting position.

Auxiliary Exercises

Keep in mind that the muscle regions and exercises mentioned are those that should be emphasized during baseball weight training. It is recommended that a player develops strength throughout his entire body. Developing the chest region, biceps, and triceps

Wrist rolls can be performed at the end of each workout.

is important to overall strength. These muscle regions should be included in the workout program as well.

Also, there are many alternative exercises not mentioned in this book that are effective for the same muscle regions. It is certainly within the right of the athlete to substitute exercises he feels are more productive. It is only important that his training program is comprehensive and strengthens the entire body.

Following is a list of auxiliary exercises that work muscle regions that are essential to overall strength. Seek the guidance of a certified trainer to make sure you are performing these exercises with proper technique.

- **Chest region**—flat bench press, incline bench press, dips, flat bench butterflies, push-ups
- **Bicep region**—bicep curls, reverse bicep curls, hammer curls, preacher curls, concentration curls

- **Tricep region**—tricep push-downs, tricep pull-downs, skull crushers, bench dips, dumbbell tricep curls
- **Legs and midsection**—power cleans, dead lifts, box steps, jump squats, leg curls

Bench press (chest region), hammer curls (bicep region), and tricep pull-downs (tricep region) are three examples of auxiliary exercises for strength training.

Sample Programs

Provided here are two programs that you can potentially follow. As mentioned, there are many comprehensive strength programs that are very productive. The player should consult a trainer to tailor a program that is suited for him, his needs, and his personal availability.

Program 1 entails four sessions per week. The athlete will perform multiple exercises for two different specific muscle regions during each of the first three workouts. During the fourth workout, he will do circuit training and extended abdominal and forearm exercises.

PROGRAM 1

Day 1: Monday—Back and Biceps

Exercise	Sets	Repetitions
Lat pull-downs (forward grip)	3	10, 10, 8
Lat pull-downs (reverse grip)	3	10, 10, 8
Seated rows	3	10, 10, 8
Pull-ups	3	10, 8, 6
Bicep curls	3	10, 10, 8
Hammer curls	3	10, 10, 8
Preacher curls	3	10, 10, 8
Concentration curls	3	10, 10, 8
Wrist rolls	4	4, 4, 3, 3
Sit-ups	4	40, 40, 30, 30

Day 2: Wednesday—Legs and Triceps

Squats	3	10, 8, 6
Standing calf raises	3	10, 10, 8
Lunges	3	10, 10, 10
Leg extensions	3	10, 10, 8
Tricep pull-downs (forward grip)	3	10, 10, 8
Tricep pull-downs (reverse grip)	3	10, 10, 8
Skull crushers	3	10, 8, 6
Bench dips	3	15, 12, 10
Forearm curls	4	10, 10, 10, 10
Elbow-to-knee sit-ups	3	40, 40, 30, 30

Day 3: Friday—Chest and Shoulders

Flat bench press	3	10, 8, 6
Incline dumbbell press	3	10, 10, 8
Dips	3	15, 12, 10
Push-ups	3	25, 25, 20
Dumbbell shoulder press	3	10, 10, 8
Standing flies	3	10, 10, 8
Lateral raises	3	10, 10, 10

Rotator cuff exercises	3	10, 10, 10
Reverse forearm curls	4	10, 10, 10, 10
Leg lifts	5	30-second intervals

Day 4: Saturday—Circuit Training

Seated calf raises	2	15, 10
Leg curls	2	15, 10
One-arm dumbbell rows	2	15, 10
Upright rows	2	15, 10
Flat bench butterflies	2	15, 10
Reverse bicep curls	2	15, 10
Dumbbell tricep curls	2	15, 10
Sit-ups	4	40, 40, 30, 30
Elbow-to-knee sit-ups	4	20, 20, 15, 15
Leg lifts	3	30-second intervals
Wrist rolls	4	4, 4, 3, 3
Forearm curls	3	10, 10, 10

A player should feel free to interchange exercises if he feels it's better for his personal workout. As he progresses, he should continue to add weight. He may also opt to increase weight and lower the number of repetitions in sets.

Program 2 also entails four sessions per week. The athlete will perform upper- and lower-body training on the same day. In addition to this program, he must do abdominal and forearm exercises at the end of each session.

PROGRAM 2

Days 1 and 3

Exercise	Sets	Repetitions
Flat bench press	5	8, 6, 4, 2, 1
Wide grip lat pull-downs	4	8, 8, 8, 8
Dumbbell shoulder press	5	8, 6, 4, 2, 1
Lunges	4	10, 8, 8, 6
Incline dumbbell bench press	5	8, 6, 4, 2, 1
Standing calf raises	4	15, 15, 15, 15
T-bar rows	4	8, 8, 8, 8

Days 2 and 4

Squats	5	10, 8, 6, 4, 2
Leg press	5	10, 8, 6, 4, 2
Bicep curls	4	12, 10, 8, 6
Skull crushers	5	12, 10, 8, 6, 2

Hammer curls	4	12, 10, 8, 6
Dumbbell tricep curls	4	12, 10, 8, 6
Leg curls	5	10, 8, 6, 4, 2

Top 10 All-Time Career Home Run Leaders

Hank Aaron	755
Barry Bonds*	734
Babe Ruth	714
Willie Mays	660
Sammy Sosa	588
Frank Robinson	586
Mark McGwire	583
Harmon Killebrew	573
Rafael Palmeiro	569
Ken Griffey Jr.*, Reggie Jackson (tie)	563

* Active player

4
Defense

Great defensive players are coveted. They help keep runs off the scoreboard and runners off base; they get the pitcher off the mound and their teammates up to bat. Good team defense wins baseball games. Like former major league player Rocky Bridges once said, "If you don't catch the ball, you catch the bus."

Hitting and pitching garner the lion's share of attention. Line drives and blazing fastballs are sexy. Offense can carry a team to an extent, but better competition will eventually expose a mediocre defensive unit. Pitching can dominate hitting, but a pitcher must have the support of the teammate in front of him and the seven behind him. Nolan Ryan, the greatest strikeout pitcher of all time, averaged 9.55 strikeouts per game. That means in contests he pitched, more than 17 outs per game were recorded by his defense. Even Nolan Ryan and his 98-mile-per-hour fastball needed the help of his defense to win 324 career games.

As baseball author and college coach Randy Voorhees states, "During games, players spend 90 percent of their time with a glove on their hand. The other time is spent at the plate or on base. Yet, players want to spend all their practice time hitting. Give me the guy who can catch the ball and throw it accurately. I want that guy on my team."

There are several variables that factor into becoming an excellent defensive player. The first step is making a commitment to take pride in your defense. Hitters have pride, and pitchers have pride. Taking pride in your defensive game will spearhead your quest to become great with the glove.

Versatility is very important and attractive to coaches at higher levels. It increases a player's value and makes him a more complete player. A player who pigeonholes himself to learning and playing just one position is making a mistake. The ability to play various positions increases a player's chances of contacting the field.

Great defensive players have value far beyond what shows up in the box score.

Another step is assessing physical strengths and matching them with a position that requires those skills. With that, identifying areas of physical weakness is also important. Players must be honest in determining their weaknesses and if they create obstacles too significant to overcome. For example, a high school player who is 5′6″ is not going to be a first baseman, nor will a player with below-average running speed play center field. This chapter addresses the physical tools necessary for each position.

As perennial all-star second baseman Roberto Alomar once said, "To me, quick feet make quick hands. If you can move your feet quickly around the bag, your hands will move quicker at the same time." Positioning and footwork are tremendous factors in defensive play. They contribute to increased range, fielding balls cleanly, and getting rid of the ball as quickly as possible. In order to showcase those good hands, players have to get to the ball by using their feet. Intelligent positioning, proper footwork on specific plays, and throwing will be discussed in this chapter.

Finally, players must be able to build their knowledge and understanding of the game so they're able to anticipate in the field. Instinct is a tremendous weapon on defense, and players who are able to anticipate plays before they happen create more opportunities to secure or steal outs.

Our program is predicated on pitching and defense. I find that if a young man is talented enough to play defense at the level and speed we require, then he is usually athletic enough to make adjustments and improvements on the offensive side of the ball.

—George Horton, head baseball coach, Cal State University, Fullerton

Versatility

From the early days of Little League baseball, the more athletic players man the infield positions, while the lesser skilled players are sent to the outfield. That's the basic trend. With the majority of hits failing to leave the infield in youth league play, it's sensible for coaches to place their best defensive players in the infield spots.

With there being less action in the outfield and the stigma that accompanies playing there, young players shy away from learning to play outfield. That is a mistake. Becoming familiar and adequate playing outfield is highly recommended, if for no other reason than there are *three* outfield positions. To crack the starting lineup as an outfielder, a player has to be in the top three on his team. There is only one catcher, one shortstop, and one first baseman. To start at those positions, the player has to be at the top of the list.

Players should make it their objective to learn as many positions as possible. It only increases their chances of making a team and earning playing time. Their stock rises in the eyes of coaches and recruiters because they offer greater value to a team. Situations such as injuries, sickness, slumps, and dismissals arise throughout a season. Having a player who can fill different spots is critical to a coach and the team. As coach Horton notes, "If a kid is a backup first baseman and he can only play first base, he has a minimal chance of getting time. However, if the same kid is capable of playing first base, third base, right field, and left field, his chances of getting playing time will increase dramatically. I also believe that knowing the game and the responsibilities of every position will help the individual slow the game down."

Another important factor in being versatile is that a player's physical skills may be better suited for a different position at higher levels of play. Each forward step in levels of play is accompanied by a need for a superior set of skills. As a whole, batters hit the ball harder and farther, and they run faster. To combat better offensive players on defense, fielders have to be quicker, faster, and more agile, and they must have stronger arms. A good high school shortstop may not cut it at shortstop in college, but he may have a chance to be a second baseman or an outfielder. A solid college third baseman may fall short in quickness and agility in the professional ranks, but he might make a good first baseman.

"Versatility is critical for a player on defense at the college level," says Scott Bradley, Princeton University head baseball coach. "My advice to players is to make sure they are comfortable playing every spot on the field. A lot of my position players have converted from

The ability to play multiple positions enhances the stock of a player in the eyes of coaches.

their high school positions. Some of my catchers in college were high school third basemen and shortstops. Many of my outfielders were infielders in high school. We're trying to recruit the best athletes with the best actions. Where exactly they'll play is largely based on the positions available at that time. The more positions you can play, the better your chances of getting playing time early on."

Players should not wait around for their coaches to take the initiative in making them versatile. That responsibility lies on the shoulders of the player. He should request extra work before or after practice. Ask the coach, assistant coach, or teammates to hit fly balls and ground balls, to throw you balls in the dirt, and so on. A player who wants to expand his talents must take the lead and put forth the efforts necessary to evolve.

Batting practice is a great time during practice to take live balls off the bat at different positions. There is no better scenario to practice defensive play than live batting practice. The ball coming off the bat from a pitch in batting practice simulates precisely how it will come off the bat in a game. Taking fungoes is good, but fielding during batting practice is better.

After taking some balls at their primary position, infielders can head to the outfield to shag fly balls, work on drop steps, and catch balls on the run. Outfielders can move to the infield and take ground balls. If you're a right fielder, move over to left field for the last 10 minutes of batting practice. If you're a shortstop, move over to second or third base and take some balls.

Achieving versatility in the field is a feather in the cap of a ballplayer. This is not to say it is unlikely for a player to remain at his primary position throughout his baseball career. It happens often. This is simply a heads-up to aspiring players to avoid putting all their eggs in one basket. There are a lot of talented players who will be competing to achieve similar aspirations. Being a versatile defensive player may provide an edge in securing a spot on the roster.

Assessing Yourself

By going back to the chart in Chapter 1, players can get some understanding of what tools are essential at specific positions. Let's take another look at how the tools are ranked for each position by professional scouts:

- **Catcher**—field, throw, bat, power, run
- **First base**—bat, power, field, throw, run
- **Second base**—bat, field, run, power, throw
- **Shortstop**—field, throw, run, bat, power
- **Third base**—bat, power, field, throw, run
- **Left field**—bat, power, run, field, throw
- **Center field**—run, field, bat, throw, power
- **Right field**—bat, power, field, throw, run

Keep in mind that this rating sheet is tailored more toward college and professional baseball. The higher the level of play, the greater the emphasis placed on position players having these skills. There are exceptions to the rule, but coaches are generally looking for certain roles out of each position. The roles for each position at younger levels of play are less defined, but if an individual player is looking to take his baseball career as far as possible, he should seriously consider factoring in this chart when selecting his primary position.

Notice how offense factors into the equation. The first and third basemen, for example, are looked upon to supply offense and power in the lineup. Corner outfielders are also positions where offense is at a premium. The middle-of-the-field catcher, shortstop, second base, and center field is where the best defensive players are found. They receive the most action in a game and have to cover the most territory.

Players have to be honest when selecting their position. An important distinction must be made between a player's favorite position and his best position. A left-handed player might love catching, but he's not going to be behind the plate for very long in his career. It's a position for right-handers. A quick, sure-handed infielder may love shortstop, but if he doesn't have a strong throwing arm, he's going to be a second baseman. Honesty can be difficult to accept at times, but the game and what's needed from each position has been around much longer than any one individual.

Good shortstops have the ability to keep their feet moving when fielding ground balls.

The specific skills I look for on the defensive side depends on the position. But in general, I look for players who are athletic, have good agility and body control, showcase quickness, and have soft hands. Athleticism is very important, and I like it when amateur baseball players also compete in other sports. It helps with their overall athleticism. Couldn't you just see Derek Jeter playing point guard?

—Mike Garlotti, scout, Colorado Rockies

Here is a more detailed description of the defensive skills that coaches would like each position player to possess:

- **Catcher**—excellent defensive skills; ability to receive pitches well, providing the pitcher with comfort and confidence in his battery mate; strong arm; quick release; quick and agile footwork; understanding of the game; strong leadership skills
- **First baseman**—height; soft hands and excellent receiving skills; quick feet; accurate throwing arm; preferably left-handed
- **Second baseman**—quickness (feet and hands); speed and agility; soft hands; good balance; ability to anticipate well; accurate throwing arm
- **Shortstop**—quickness (feet and hands); speed and agility; smooth and fluid fielding through the ball; aggressive; soft hands; good balance; ability to anticipate well; strong and accurate throwing arm; ability to throw on the move; good leadership skills
- **Third baseman**—quick reactions; soft hands; aggressive; ability to throw on the run; strong and accurate arm; ability to anticipate well
- **Left fielder**—quickness and speed; accurate throwing arm; good judgment on balls in the air; ability to go back on balls; ability to consistently field ground balls
- **Center fielder**—speed; strong leadership skills; aggressiveness; fearlessness; good judgment on balls in the air; ability to go back and come in on balls; ability to anticipate well; ability to consistently field ground balls

A good first baseman makes the entire infield better.

- **Right fielder**—strong throwing arm; good judgment on balls in the air; ability to go back on balls; ability to consistently field ground balls

Some of these skills are considered god-given. A strong arm, great speed, and quickness are all physical traits that some players are born with, while others fall short. There is no question that genetics and physiological makeup are strong contributors to some skills. However, all of the aforementioned physical skills can be improved. Perfecting technique and training can improve power, speed, and quickness. With that, several of the characteristics listed as necessities for each position are not innate. Many are developed through proper technique and repetitious training.

SKILLS THAT ARE GOD-GIVEN BUT CAN BE IMPROVED
- Running speed
- Quickness
- Agility

- Arm strength
- Reaction time
- General strength
- Natural athleticism (coordination, explosiveness, and fluidity)

SKILLS THAT ARE DEVELOPED THROUGH PROPER TECHNIQUE AND REPETITIOUS TRAINING

- Soft hands
- Quick release
- Throwing accuracy
- Judgment
- Ability to anticipate
- Aggressiveness
- Fearlessness
- Leadership skills
- Understanding of the game

It's when these two categories are combined that outstanding defensive players evolve. Regardless of what god-given abilities are bestowed upon each individual, he should focus his efforts on becoming the very best he can be in each of these areas.

Advanced Defensive Play

It is never good to assume, but for the purposes of this book and its audience, the author presumes players are already able to execute the basic fundamentals of catching, fielding a ground ball, and tracking down fly balls. (Throwing form will be discussed in Chapter 5.) Instead of addressing the rudimentary defensive skills, plays of greater difficulty will be covered. The routine plays should be practiced regularly, but five-tool players need to carry a full bag of tricks out onto the field.

Positioning

Casual baseball fans complain that the game is too slow. Teams change from offense to defense a minimum of 17 times, time elapses between each pitch, and the ball is in play for only brief periods of time. But that time between pitches is when players lay down their swords and put on their thinking caps. Batters adjust their plan of attack between each pitch and formulate an educated guess as to what pitch is coming next. Pitchers assess the batter, the count, the game situation, and their "stuff" to determine what pitch they'll throw next and where they'll throw it.

And fielders? They had better be thinking right along with the play and taking their position according to what they observe and anticipate. Cal Ripken Jr. is considered one of the finest shortstops ever to play the game. His speed and quickness were average at best by major league standards, but his range was outstanding. Ripken was notorious for always being in the right spot. He was able to do this because he studied opposing hitters, understood how his pitchers were going to attack them, and factored in the count and game situation before each pitch. Fastening all of those pieces into the puzzle determined whether Ripken would shift two steps to the left or three to the right, move a step in or two back, or remain in the same spot.

Moving those couple steps can make all the difference in the world. A runner may be safe by a half step or out by a half step depending on whether a defensive player was in good position or out of position, respectively. A fly ball is caught for an out or lands safely for a double depending on whether the outfielder did his homework between pitches or stood there dazed in the same spot for three straight hitters. Players who anticipate the play are the ones that make the plays.

Luck is the residue of design.

—Branch Rickey, baseball sage and former major league
scout and general manager

Field and Weather Conditions

During pregame, a player should take account of the field and weather conditions. Both play a role in defensive positioning. Take note of the following variables and how they can impact play.

To make the advanced play, defensive players need to anticipate so they're able to get into position in a timely fashion.

WIND. Wind is especially important to outfielders since they catch most of the balls that are hit in the air. With the wind blowing in toward the batter, outfielders can afford to play shallower. Fly balls will be knocked down and deep fly balls will hang up in the air for a longer period of time. When the wind blows out, outfielders need to play deeper. They also have to know the ball will carry more, so when they're giving chase, the ball will travel farther than originally thought when it leaves the bat.

Infielders should also pay attention to the wind, especially when it's blowing in. Short fly balls may hold up and become the responsibility of the infielder. Infielders should always go after pop-ups and short fly balls as if it's theirs to catch until they hear the outfielder call them off.

Crosswinds also influence ball flight. If the wind is blowing from right field to left field, for example, fly balls hit to right field will hang up, balls hit to center field will drift toward left, and balls hit to left field will hook or slice more drastically. Infielders must factor in crosswinds before calling for the ball as well as when the ball's in foul territory. (Balls may stay in play.)

SUN. Players should be cognizant of where the sun is throughout the game. They should know they'll have to shield their eyes from the sun (with their glove) before it's hit into the air. Outfielders must have sunglasses (if they own them) at their disposal throughout the entire game. There are times when the sun is not a factor for the right fielder in the first inning but is by the sixth inning.

When a fly ball is hit and the sun is in the fielder's eyes, he should first block the sun with his glove and then find the ball. A player can also adjust the angle of his body (and eyes) on his approach to the catch so that the sun becomes less of a factor.

DIRT. The ball slows down when the infield dirt is soft or wet. Infielders may have to take a step or two in when playing on soft or sandy dirt. Also, they've got to stay down on ground balls because

Outfielders must factor in the wind before the ball is hit so they're able to run to the right spot.

the ball is less likely to come up (bounce). When the dirt is hard (especially if there is a long stretch without rain), infielders should play deeper. Ground balls will travel faster and fielders may need that extra distance to maintain their range. Shortstops and third basemen should bear in mind that playing deeper also means they'll have to make a longer throw.

GRASS. The higher the grass, the longer it takes for the ball to get through the infield. Players have to shorten up, especially when there is a fast runner or left-handed hitter at the plate. Short grass has a lesser impact.

Wet grass also slows the ball down. In addition, the ball may be slippery by the time it gets into the throwing hand. If the ball is very wet, fielders may have to go to a three-finger grip to ensure accuracy.

Hitter-Pitcher Matchup

Who stands at the plate is a major factor in positioning. Middle-of-the-lineup hitters tend to have more power, so the defense may back up a little in anticipation of a ball being hit hard or deep. Leadoff and bottom-of-the-lineup hitters are typically less powerful but may possess speed. The defense may have to shorten up their positioning. There are always exceptions to the rule, but understanding customary roles of hitters in the lineup is a general starting point when anticipating on defense.

A hitter's swing can also help players defend the field. A right-handed hitter, for example, may cast his hands out and get around the ball on every swing. The defense should shift to their right and play for pulled balls. The next right-handed hitter may let the ball get really deep in the hitting zone and use an inside-out swing (barrel drags behind the handle) to drive the ball to the opposite field. Fielders should shift to their left in this situation.

The pitcher on the mound also has a say in where balls are likely to be hit. Is the pitcher throwing blazing fastballs that hitters have trouble catching up to? If so, fielders should shade a couple steps toward the opposite field. Is the pitcher throwing a lot of off-speed pitches attempting to fool hitters and get them out on their front foot? In this case, fielders should shade toward the pull-side and slightly in.

Pay strict attention to takes, swings and misses, and foul balls for each hitter. They can tell you a lot about a hitter's timing. With that, keep track of what the hitter has done in his previous at-bats or games.

Lastly, pay attention to pitch sequences, what signal the catcher is putting down, and where he's setting up. This is essential to anticipating the direction of the hit on each pitch. Hard fastball away? Shade to the opposite field. Changeup? Shade to the pull-side. Continue to read the hitter's swing and his timing, the pitcher and his pitches, and the catcher's signals and setup.

Remember, all of this information is critical to infielders and outfielders. Mistakes by outfielders, either fielding or positioning, carry a much greater penalty than blips by infielders. As Tim McCarver states, "Outfield positioning is more important than infield positioning because outfielders have much more room to cover."

Game Situation

The shortstop has factored in the wind, the density of the dirt, and the height of the grass, and he knows that the sun is behind him. He recognizes that the hitter is opening up and trying to pull everything and that the catcher just called for a changeup. Now is he prepared to position himself? Not quite.

There happens to be a runner on first base, and there are two outs in the inning. With this in mind, the shortstop can play a step or two deeper. Because he has a shorter throw with there being a force play at second base, he can move back a little to increase his range. This is an example of factoring in the game situation. Here are a few more situations that require a position player to adjust where he takes his ready position:

FIRST BASEMAN

> **Runner on first base.** Hold the runner on first.
>
> **Runners on first and second base.** Play just behind the runner to keep him honest, or play deep behind the runner. Or play on the grass in front of the runner in a bunt situation.

Bases loaded. Play up on the grass if going for the force-out, just behind the base if looking to turn a 3-6-3 double play, or deep if just looking to get an out.

Runner on third base, close game. Play up on the grass or even with the base with fewer than two outs.

Runners on first and third base. Hold the runner or play just behind the runner.

Last inning, close game. Play a step or two closer to the line to defend against the extra-base hit.

SECOND BASEMAN

Runner on first base. Play two steps in and two steps toward second base for double-play depth. Also, cover for the steal.

Runner on second base. Play shaded slightly toward second base to keep the runner at second honest with his lead.

Runner on third base. Play on the grass, halfway (even with second base), or back, depending on the inning and score.

Bases loaded. Play up on the grass or at double-play depth, depending on the inning, score, and speed of the batter.

With runners on first and second base, the first baseman often plays behind the runner to increase his range but still keep the runner honest.

SHORTSTOP

Runner on first base. Play two steps in and two steps toward second base for double-play depth. Also, cover for the steal.

Runner on second base. Play shaded slightly toward second base to keep the runner at second honest with his lead.

Runner on third base. Play on the grass, halfway (even with second base), or back, depending on the inning and score.

Bases loaded. Play up on the grass or at double-play depth, depending on the inning, score, and speed of the batter.

Force at second, two outs. Play a couple of steps deep with shorter throw to second for the force.

THIRD BASEMAN

Runner on first base. Play even or slightly behind third base, and step closer to second base for the double play. Also, cheat up on the grass in a bunt situation.

Runners on first and second base. Play even or slightly behind third base, and step closer to second base for the double play. In a bunt situation, play slightly in front of third base, with the left

Up by a run late in the game, the third baseman plays deep and toward the line to defend the extra-base hit. The purpose is to keep the tying run off second base.

foot dropped back, to view the runner on second to make sure he doesn't attempt to steal.

Bases loaded. Play up on the grass if going for the force at home, even with the bag if looking to turn a 5-4-3 double play or deep if just looking for an out. Also, there is the option of a 5-3 unassisted double play.

Last inning, close game. Play deeper and shade toward the line to prevent the extra-base hit.

OUTFIELDER

Leading by one or two runs, late in the game. Play deep to prevent an extra-base hit.

Runner on third base, fewer than two outs. Play at normal depth or in to have a chance to throw the runner out at home plate.

Runner on second base, close score late in the game. Play shallower to have a chance at throwing the runner out at home on a base hit.

Footwork

Having great hands is an attribute generally regarded as integral to being a good defensive player. But the very best players possess exceptional footwork when it comes to executing the toughest plays

---

How an Offense Might Tip the Bunt

- Third base coach calls extra attention to himself and goes through a sequence of signs.
- Batter moves up in the box.
- Batter moves closer to home plate.
- Base runners seem more attentive and intense on the base.
- Batter chokes up or demonstrates something different in his stance position—for example, stands more upright.
- Players in the dugout become more alert, whisper to each other, or become dead quiet.
- Batter appears disenchanted when viewing the signs.

---

on the field. "The feet dictate what the rest of your body does," says Chris Pittaro, former major league infielder. "When developing players on defense, we work from the ground up. Quickness and agility allow you to get to and field balls, but with that, balance and footwork are so important to arm strength, throwing on the run, and throwing from different angles."

Improving speed, quickness, and agility helps players at every position on the field. Those traits are discussed in detail in Chapter 6. Applying those traits to proper footwork is how infielders and outfielders make the difficult plays appear routine. Players need to isolate and practice proper footwork on these plays so they maintain balance and perform instinctively.

DROP STEPS. A drop step is the first step a defensive player takes when tracking down a ball hit over his head. Because infielders and outfielders have to go back on balls during games, both should practice drop steps.

From the ready position, the player reads the ball off the bat. If the ball is hit over his right shoulder, for example, he opens his hips by dropping his right foot back. He "points his toe to where he wants to go." The player turns his back to the ball and runs to the spot where he feels the ball will fall. As he runs back, he intermittently glances over his left shoulder to check the ball and its whereabouts.

If he has time, he gets around the ball and catches the ball with two hands over his throwing shoulder. If he has to catch the ball on the run, he reaches up with his glove only to receive the ball. On balls hit over the player's left shoulder, he takes a drop step with his left foot.

On balls hit directly over their heads, players have to determine if they prefer catching the ball on their glove side or their throwing side when going back on the ball, for the following reason. They are going to take a drop step to one side (whichever they prefer) and then bow out on their path back to the ball. This pushes the ball to one side, rather than running directly under it. A right-handed player who prefers to catch the ball on his glove side would drop step with his left foot, arc out slightly to the left, and receive the ball on his glove side.

On balls hit over his head, the outfielder takes an initial drop step before running to the point of the ball's descent.

DOUBLE-PLAY TURNS. A shortstop making a double-play turn on a feed from the second baseman must get to the base quickly. He should run toward the back corner of the base. Although he wants to have momentum toward first base as he receives the ball, the shortstop must have controlled momentum as he accepts the throw from the second baseman. If he approaches the base with too much speed and the throw is off-line, he'll have difficulty securing one out let alone turning two.

As the ball is received, the shortstop swipes the rear corner of the base. Umpires allow infielders to cheat on double-play turns to evade the runner, so he can even slide his foot just behind the corner. The shortstop should swing his rear end around hard to the left to have balance and momentum going toward first base on his throw. Often, shortstops fail to control their balance and are fading toward right field, resulting in weaker, less accurate throws.

When receiving the throw, always reach for the ball, catch it with two hands, and catch it in the palm. Catching the ball in the web makes it more difficult to dig out on the transfer from glove to throwing hand.

On turns when the feed is coming from the first baseman, the shortstop holds the back or outside of second base with his right foot if the first baseman fields the ball behind the runner. This gives him a clear throwing lane. If the first baseman fields the ball in front of

The shortstop gets to the back of the base, and as he receives the ball with two hands, he drags his right foot behind the base before making the throw to first.

the runner, the shortstop holds the inside of the base with his left foot.

On throws from the pitcher and catcher, the shortstop should always go to the front of the base with his left foot. He receives the ball sooner and takes the base out of the equation on low throws.

Second basemen have multiple double-play pivots they can employ. The first is the most efficient but the most dangerous. The player straddles the base, his left foot on the first-base side of the base and his right foot on the opposite side. He receives the throw, rocks to his back foot, and throws. After the throw, he must leap up off his left foot to avoid the incoming runner. This is the quickest transfer but places the second baseman in a vulnerable position to the base runner.

Another (safer) turn is to come across the base. The second baseman steps on the base with his left foot, comes across the base to the third-base side when the ball is thrown, and receives the ball as he lands on his right foot. (His shoulders should be aligned with first base as he receives the ball.) He quickly transfers the ball from glove to hand, takes a jab step with his left foot, and fires to first base. This turn is best used on ground balls to third base and balls to deep short.

The second baseman can also receive the ball at the back of the base, step back toward right-center field and throw to first. Here, he gently steps on the base with his left foot. As the ball is received, he pushes off the base with his left foot, lands on the ball of his right foot, aligns his shoulders to first base, steps and throws. This turn is best used on balls that the shortstop fields to his left.

DOUBLE-PLAY FEEDS. The opportunity to turn a double play only happens when there is a quick, accurate feed. A shortstop has an easier feed because his feet are already aligned as he fields the ball.

When the shortstop sets himself to field the ball, he should position his right foot slightly ahead of his left foot. He should attempt to field the ball off-center to his right. As he fields the ball, he brings his glove toward the throwing position and gets the ball out of his glove as quickly as possible. This helps the second baseman pick up the throw. The shortstop should stay down and think about throwing the ball uphill to the second baseman's chest. It is not necessary

When coming across the bag on a double-play turn, the second baseman steps on the base with his left foot, plants his right foot as he receives the ball with two hands, and takes a short step with his left foot to throw to first base.

to stand up, get his arm to a high release point, and throw. That takes too much time.

On balls that take him far to his left, the shortstop should use an underhand toss. Again, he should get the ball out of his glove as quickly as possible, give a firm toss to second base, and follow the toss.

Feeds are more difficult for second basemen. On balls hit directly at them, they can quickly shift and exchange their feet, drop-step with their right foot, and throw to second or drop their left knee down and turn the shoulders before throwing to the shortstop. Each second baseman must find what is comfortable and workable for him. Regardless of which technique the player uses, he should make sure he's not falling back on the throw. He should think about finishing his throw to keep his momentum forward, not back.

On balls to his right, the second baseman can execute an underhand toss or a table toss. A table toss is when the player grabs the

Here, the second baseman opens his right foot
and drops his left knee as he turns to second
base for the double-play feed. It's important to
get the throwing arm up and avoid leaning back

ball from his glove, points his right elbow toward his target, and tosses the ball with his arm moving outward from left to right. If this is practiced, it's a very effective method of releasing the ball quickly.

A ball that is hit far to the second baseman's left necessitates a reverse pivot. After gloving the ball on the move outside of his left foot, the player takes a crossover step with his right foot. He plants hard with his right foot, turns and aligns his shoulders to second base (his back is facing home plate), and fires a strike to the outside of second base.

FIELDING THROUGH THE BALL. It's very rare for Derek Jeter to show off his arm in the infield. He's very smooth and controlled coming to the ball, gloves it, and seemingly flicks the ball across the diamond over to the first base. Because he gets to the ball quickly and has momentum toward first base as he fields it, Jeter appears to catch

The right foot should be slightly ahead of the left foot when fielding a ground ball on a double-play feed from the shortstop.

and throw the ball with great ease. He is one of the best at fielding through the ball.

There is a reason why the shortstop is generally the best player on the field. Any slight blunder or bobble, and the runner will likely be safe. The shortstop is farthest from the batter, so the ball takes longer to get to him and he also has a long throw to first base. The shortstop is also involved in nearly every play during the game. He needs range, quickness, good hands, and a strong and accurate throwing arm. The shortstop must be athletic enough to field through the ball, rather than setting his feet and receiving the ball in the standard stationary fielding position.

Because the shortstop is the infielder farthest from the batter, he must go to the ball on routine hits to receive the ball sooner. This shortens the distance of his throw to first base. If he sits back and waits, fast runners will often be safe at first base.

On a routine ground ball, the shortstop first needs to approach the ball so he's fielding it with his momentum going toward first base.

This may require a step or two to the right to circle (or get around) the ball. On his approach to the ball, the final step should be with the left foot landing in front of the right foot. The shortstop fields the ball with two hands just in front of and inside his right foot. This puts his glove and throwing hand in a closer position to his release point.

When a shortstop fields through the ball, his feet should never come to a complete rest. His first two steps to the ball are big and aggressive to eat up ground. As he approaches the ball, he's got to slow down a bit to get himself under control. But his feet never stop moving, so he is able to maintain his momentum toward first base.

THROWING ON THE RUN. On slow hit balls, third basemen and short-stops have to throw on the run. Coaches often cry out to players to set their feet, but on certain plays, the defensive player must throw on the run to have a chance at the runner. Always keep in mind that for every step the infielder takes, the runner is taking two steps.

There are two methods of fielding the ball and throwing on the run. The first is to field the ball with the glove outside the left foot. This is the easier technique, though it takes a little more time to execute. The player charges the slow roller and fields the ball with just his glove outside his left foot. He then steps with his right foot (giving time to transfer the ball from glove to hand) and throws the ball as his left foot lands. The release point is between three-quarter and sidearm, and the fielder should factor in tail on his throw and aim a bit to the left of the target.

The more advanced method of fielding and throwing on the run is to field the ball just inside the right foot. The defensive player takes his final step with his left foot forward and gloves the ball with two hands inside his right foot. As his right foot lands on his next step, he throws the ball from the three-quarter or sidearm position.

It is absolutely necessary for the player to field the ball with two hands when attempting this technique. The ball has to be fielded and transferred to the throwing hand immediately in order for him to release the ball by the time his right foot lands.

Throwing off the wrong foot (the right foot) takes practice, and shortstops and third basemen should work on it routinely. There is a rhythm to this technique that takes time to perfect.

THROWING TO SECOND ON STEALS. A strong arm and quick release are skills that catchers should focus on in order to consistently throw out base runners attempting to steal. Without quick and efficient footwork, however, those quality skills will be deemed useless.

College recruiters and professional scouts measure catcher throws to second base with a stopwatch. The major league average pop-to-pop time is between 1.8 and 2.0 seconds. There are three basic methods of footwork used for throwing to second base on a steal. Catchers may employ the technique they find to be most suitable.

- **Jump pivot method.** The jump pivot is the most commonly used method by catchers. As the ball is received, the catcher quickly shifts his feet. Then the right foot shifts clockwise (slightly back and to the left) and lands so it points toward

Fielding on the run and throwing off the wrong foot may provide the only chance at getting the runner on a slow roller.

the first-base dugout. This aligns the feet and shoulders to the target. The catcher takes a short jab step with his left and fires to second base. This all should take less than a second.

- **Two-step method.** As the ball is received, the catcher takes a step out to the right. He then steps forward with the left foot toward second base and fires to the base. This technique is conditional. First, it's only used when there is a right-handed batter at the plate. Second, it's mostly used on pitches to the middle and outside part of home plate. The release time takes longer on pitches to the inside part of the plate.
- **Rocker step method.** This method is for catchers possessing above-average arms. As the ball is received, the catcher rocks back on his right foot, squares his shoulders, takes a short step with his left foot, and throws. This technique offers the quickest release, but a catcher must have excellent arm strength to cut down the runner.

Footwork at the catcher's position becomes more and more important to throwing out runners at higher levels of play.

The All-Time Fielding Percentage Leaders by Position

1b	Don Mattingly	.996
2b	Roberto Alomar	.985
3b	Brooks Robinson	.971
SS	Omar Vizquel*	.984
OF	Amos Otis	.991
OF	Terry Puhl	.993
OF	Joe Rudi	.991
C	Elston Howard	.993
P	Jim Kaat, Greg Maddux* (tie)	16 Gold Gloves

* Active player

5
Arm Strength

Standing in front of you are two 17-year-old baseball players. The first player looks like a well-conditioned athlete. He owns an impressive résumé of playing experience, competes in games eight months out of the year, and has exceptional throwing mechanics.

The second player is lanky with no muscle tone. He plays baseball in the spring for recreational purposes only and never trains outside of team practices during the season. He has little to no guidance or training, and his throwing form is flawed.

The two players stand on flat ground, each holding a baseball. The seasoned baseball player steps and throws at maximum velocity. The radar gun reads 75 miles per hour. The recreational player steps and throws at his maximum velocity. The radar gun reads 79 miles per hour.

How is this possible? How can an individual with practically no training or teaching and limited game experience possibly throw a ball harder than a polished, conditioned student of the game? The answer is that certain individuals are the beneficiary of physiological and genetic traits that enable them to move their arm at a faster rate than others. That is the answer in its simplest form. The fact that Billy Wagner, standing at 5'10", can throw a ball 100 miles per hour is not because he has found some secret that only a handful of human beings have access to. Wagner is blessed with a great arm. As catcher Crash Davis, the character played by Kevin Costner in the classic baseball movie *Bull Durham*, put it to his young prospect pitcher Nuke Laloosh, "You've got a gift. When you were a baby the gods reached down and turned your right arm into a lightning bolt."

Arm strength is a combination of technique, conditioning, and physiological makeup.

Wagner has worked hard to refine his throwing mechanics and condition his body and arm to maximize the potential of that blessed throwing arm, but he was given a gift. The percentage of working fast-twitch muscle fibers in his left arm exceeds the average number found in the common man.

Players, coaches, and parents often have difficulty grasping this concept. While tutelage and training can improve a player's arm strength to the highest possible level that he is capable of reaching (which is the purpose of this book), he may never reach the level of certain teammates or opponents.

It's much like running speed, jumping ability (vertical leap), or general strength. Much of it is innate. Many fathers will accept the fact that their sons are slow-footed but can't comprehend why they don't throw the ball harder. It's the same concept. Why are some students exceptional in mathematics but struggle writing a term paper? Why are some people very calm and unflappable while others are high-octane and anxious? It's the way we're wired. Former major league pitcher and author Tom House mentions in his book *The Pitching Edge*, "Arm speed is genetic. Training arm strength and endurance will only support the fast-twitch muscle tissue with which the pitcher was born."

As mentioned, the purpose of this book is to survey each baseball tool and streamline efforts into attaining optimum performance. Arm strength can be improved. Proper throwing technique and training programs will help players reach those levels.

Having a good arm in the field has great benefits. On a tough play, it can help a player throw out a runner who would have otherwise been safe had the throw instead come from a player with a mediocre arm. It can allow a shortstop or right fielder to play deeper to increase their range without sacrificing their ability to throw a runner out. It can make up for a bobbled ball or taking a poor route to the ball by putting more zip on the throw and beating the runner to the base.

Great arm strength can also be of assistance to an individual and team without the player's even having to throw the ball. How is that? When a catcher has an exceptional throw to second base, it can shut down the opposition's running game. An opposing coach may not even flash the steal sign because he determines it's too risky. Much like with a runner on second base and the batter sending a clean

A strong throwing arm enables fielders to finish off a great play.

single to right field, the third base coach holds the runner because he saw how good the right fielder's arm looked in warm-ups. That is the ultimate respect, and when a player can stop a team from advancing bases without even throwing the ball, he adds true value to a team's defense.

A good arm gives the player a chance to record an out when confronted with the game's more advanced plays. Turning a double play, fielding a slow roller and throwing on the run, throwing out a runner who is tagging, or taking a relay throw from the outfield and gunning a runner down at the plate—players with average or below-average arms have a tougher time making these plays. A strong arm finishes off these plays, which can provide a momentum shift in the game.

A final reason arm strength assists a player is that he is boundless with regard to what position he can play. Size, speed, quickness, and agility are also factors, but having a strong arm keeps a player in the mix of playing any position. A weak arm limits a player's options on the defensive side of the ball. Typically, players who have below-average arms will be relegated to second base, left field, or first base. They are very rarely found playing shortstop, catcher, third base, or right field. A good arm can only help a player's chances when being evaluated for specific positions.

How Arm Strength Is Assessed

Assessing arm strength is a fairly easy read. Common sense is enough to distinguish players who have a strong arm from those possessing a weak arm. The ball either leaves the player's arm with life or it does not. Other factors, such as the fluidity of a player's throwing motion, come into play when observing a player. Does his motion appear to be effortless or strenuous? Also, does the player's throw have good carry? A great arm produces throws that maintain their speed and path to the target for long periods of time, as opposed to cutting or fading midway through flight.

Arm strength is typically assessed visually by college recruiters and professional scouts. Using a radar gun reading is extremely rare (and, to a point, unnecessary) when evaluating a position player. Pregame infield and outfield practice is the time when scouts like to assess arm strength because there is no guarantee they'll see a player max out on a throw during the game. With this in mind, it's important for aspiring players to show off their arms during infield or outfield practice. Let it go. You never know who is watching. In addition, throwing the ball at maximum velocity during pregame may deter base coaches and players from attempting to take extra bases during the game.

When assessing arm strength, I obviously look at the pace of the throw. Is the ball thrown on a line or is there arc to it? Is the player getting proper rotation on the ball so it carries? Is the infielder able to throw the ball from different arm angles? To get a good rating, the player has to have a strong arm. There's not a whole lot of projecting, because arm strength is a tool that doesn't improve much after high school.

—John Wilson, area scout, Minnesota Twins

Infielders

True arm strength is best displayed when a player has to throw the ball after making a backhand play. This position allows the player to gain little, if any, momentum toward his target. A player with an above-average arm is able to throw the ball across the infield on a line with exceptional velocity. The throw will have carry through the bag. A player with an average arm is able to throw the ball to the base on a line with some "life" on the throw. How much life or pop is on the throw is somewhat subjective, but it is not difficult to identify by scouts and recruiters who have observed thousands of players. Players with a below-average arm will have some arc or trajectory on their throw.

Scouts and recruiters also consider release time when grading arms. A player with an average arm who has a quick release increases his value. Taking a long time to get rid of the ball detracts

During infield or outfield practice, a player shouldn't be afraid to show off his arm. You never know who may be watching.

from whatever arm strength a player might possess. The ability to maintain arm strength when throwing from different arm angles is as important as well. This falls in line with being able to get rid of the ball quickly.

Arm strength is something that stands out pretty easily, but I want to see that the infielder has a relaxed throwing motion and that he has simple technique. If his technique is stiff and he has some "yips" in it, he's going to have a tough time throwing on the run and adjusting his arm angle on certain throws, both of which are necessary to playing infield.

—Scott Bradley, former major league player and head baseball coach,
Princeton University

Outfielders

An outfielder with an average arm should be able to throw the ball from 250 feet to home plate on a line with the ball taking just one bounce. An outfielder with an above-average arm will be able to throw the ball on a line and have it skip off the ground without losing much speed. There is a difference between the ball bouncing (losing significant speed) and skipping (losing little speed) to the catcher, and it's a way to measure the outfielder's arm strength. An outfielder who throws a ball that dies as it hits the ground does not have a strong arm.

Another way an outfielder can measure himself is to get into an outfield position approximately 300 feet from home plate and have a coach hit him a clean base hit. The outfielder charges the ball, fields it, and throws home. The entire process from the ball making contact with the bat to the throw reaching the catcher's glove is timed on a stopwatch. A good baserunning time by major league averages from second base to home plate is seven seconds. If the outfielder's time is around seven seconds, his path to the ball, release time, and arm strength are comparable to what's found at the major league level. If it's far off, then he is far off by those standards.

Having four-seam rotation is also important when throwing from the outfield. Because throws are longer, any tail or cut to the ball will be magnified. Imparting straight, four-seam rotation allows the ball to travel on a straight path, which optimizes accuracy and minimizes the distance of the throw.

Players like Andruw Jones, Vladimir Guerrero, Jeff Francouer, and Ichiro Suzuki are able to throw the ball from that distance and more on a straight line to the catcher without having to bounce the ball. These players are very rare and possess exceptional arm strength even by major league standards.

Catchers

A catcher's arm strength is measured by his pop-to-pop time. The stopwatch starts when the ball hits the catcher's glove (pop) and stops when the ball hits the infielder's glove (pop) at second base. Catchers with good times combine arm strength and a quick release. A good pop-to-pop time for a catcher is between 1.8 and 2.0 sec-

Because he has the longest throw to third base, the right fielder typically has the strongest arm in the outfield.

onds. Anything below 1.8 is exceptional. Anything above 2.0 makes the catcher dependent on the pitcher having a quick delivery to the plate or the base runner running a slower time to second base.

Improving Arm Strength

While genetics factor into the arm strength of each individual player, there are components that enable players to improve and realize their maximum arm speed and throwing accuracy. Refining throwing mechanics, resistance training, and throwing programs are areas that assist players in improving their throwing arm. According to Richard Rembielak, head baseball coach at Wake Forest University, "Proper technique goes a long way. Having flexibility and full range of motion in the arm enhances arm strength. Exercises that help in developing those two characteristics will improve arm strength along with increasing the player's overall physical strength."

The major league average pop-to-pop time is 1.9 seconds.

Throwing Mechanics

When it comes to throwing mechanics, players often assume that it's a subject isolated to pitchers. This couldn't be farther from the truth. Proper throwing form enables position players to maximize arm strength, throw the ball accurately, and reduce the chances of arm soreness and injury. Every player on the field should address their throwing mechanics and seek improvement for these reasons.

Commonly a player's throwing form is based on how he picked up a ball and threw it when he was a very young child. Through trial and error, the player makes subtle adjustments during his developmental years to achieve greater speed and better accuracy. However, the foundation of his throwing form is often flawed. Technique can be polished by understanding proper throwing mechanics, identifying the flaws at hand, and then rebuilding new, good habits through repetitious training. A player will only realize his optimum arm strength and accuracy when he perfects his throwing mechanics. The more faults that are practiced, the more he decreases his speed and accuracy and increases the chance of soreness or injury.

GRIP. When throwing the baseball, pitchers use a variety of grips to make the ball move or change pace. In the field, there is one grip and only one grip to use. Position players should always use a four-seam grip. A four-seam grip allows the player to throw the ball as hard as possible, as straight as possible, and with carry. That is what a defensive player at every position is after each time he receives the ball and prepares to throw it.

For right-handed throwers, hold the ball so the seams form a reverse *C*. The middle and index fingers rest across the top seam so the stitches contact the upper pads of the fingers. The thumb rests against the left side of the ball, and the ring and pinkie fingers rest against the right side. (The exact opposite is true for left-handed throwers.) The only time an infielder may alter his grip is if the ground is very wet and the ball becomes slippery. In this case, he may use a three-finger grip to ensure better control of his throw.

When a player uses a four-seam grip, the ball rotates so the stitches cut through air resistance at a maximum rate. This helps the ball maintain speed, direction, and carry. If a player was using a two-seam grip (resting his fingers along or on top of the seams),

A four-seam grip gives the thrower optimum velocity, accuracy, and carry.

the smooth part of the baseball would travel through the air with greater frequency. The air or wind resistance has a greater impact on the ball's flight, which diminishes its speed, direction, and carry. Think of a pitcher throwing a two-seam fastball. He sacrifices a few miles per hour of velocity to gain movement on the pitch. From the infield and outfield, players don't want movement nor do they want to reduce velocity.

Players should employ a four-seam grip every time they remove the ball from their glove, whether they're playing catch, fielding ground balls, or tossing the ball up to themselves. Over time, a player's hand will automatically search for and find a four-seam grip without him having to give it any thought. It will become habit.

The grip should be firm but not too tight. The player should allow some space between the ball and the palm of his hand. The ball should not be jammed into the palm or gripped too tightly, as that will diminish velocity, accuracy, and carry.

ALIGNMENT AND SEPARATION. After the grip is taken, players need to align their feet, hips, and shoulders to the target. The feet and shoulders should square up to the location of the throw. Imagine taking a batting stance and the pitcher is your target.

The throw is initiated by taking a step (left foot for right-handers and vice versa) directly at the target. The step is a short, controlled stride. The foot lands pointed to the 1:00 position for right-handers and the 11:00 position for left-handers. The toe should not be pointed directly at the target, as this will open the hips and shoulders prematurely. The hips and shoulders should remain closed and aligned with the target when the stride foot lands.

As the step is taken, the throwing hand and glove hand separate. The throwing arm swings back and away from the target, while the glove swings forward toward the target. An image that helps players understand the proper glove-arm position at separation is to imagine they're wearing a wristwatch and showing their target the face of the watch. As the throwing arm swings upward, it bends at a 45-degree angle at the elbow. At the ready or power position, the ball is faced away from the target, with the wrist turned slightly inward. If a right-handed player were standing on the pitcher's mound, the

The feet and shoulders should be aligned with the target to initiate a throw.

ball would be facing the shortstop position. The shoulders are tilted slightly upward.

When practicing form throwing, players should always start with their hands together. They should have the ball in the glove, reach in to grip it, and separate from that position. Nearly every throw on the baseball field begins with the ball being taken out of the glove.

THE THROW. Once the player is in the power or ready position to throw the ball, several things happen simultaneously: the glove arm pulls inward, the throwing arm begins its motion of delivery, and

A thought to have when separating the ball from the glove is to turn the thumbs down. In the power position, the glove is held out toward the target and the throwing elbow is at or above the shoulder. Notice that the ball is faced away from the target.

the front leg stiffens. Players have to work on the rhythm or timing of their throwing motion, because if this series of movements falls out of sequence, accuracy and speed will be diminished.

To initiate the throw, the player pulls his glove arm inward. Bending at the elbow, the player tucks his glove arm in alongside his rib cage. This helps rotate and accelerate his throwing arm forward. Use of the glove arm is critical in maximizing velocity and alleviating stress on the throwing arm. Players often make the mistake of simply clearing their glove arm out of the way and generating all of their arm speed with the throwing side of their body. This reduces arm strength and increases the chance of injury.

As the glove arm is being pulled inward, the throwing arm begins its motion. The shoulder externally rotates, and the wrist and hand begin to turn toward the target. The elbow remains as high as or higher than the shoulder throughout the throw and actually leads the hands and wrist. The arm accelerates forward as the fingers remain on top of the ball.

As the elbow passes in front of the shoulders, the hand and wrist whip forward to throw the ball. The player should focus on extending his arm down the target line and firing through the ball. His throwing arm pulls down and across his body, finishing across his opposite-side hip. The momentum of his motion should force his throwing-side leg to lift up off the ground and finish in front of his stride foot.

Although the player initiates his throw with a soft, controlled stride, the front leg eventually stiffens or braces so his hips can forcefully rotate. The faster the hips rotate, the faster the throwing arm moves. The momentum built by the big muscles of the legs, abdomen, and back is transferred through the shoulders to the pitching arm and hand, enabling them to sail by the head toward the target. There is no faster human movement than this—like a whip, the throwing hand slings the ball forward.

Throughout the throwing motion, the player must remain relaxed and tension free. The muscles contract when the player tries to throw too hard, which reduces arm speed. The player should remain fluid and think of his arm as a whip. He must trust the thought that keeping tension out of the throwing motion is how he'll generate maximum arm speed.

When throwing the baseball, the player pulls the glove arm inward, which helps accelerate the throwing arm forward to the point of release. The throwing arm finishes across the opposite-side leg. Notice that the hips have rotated and the throwing-side leg is carried forward by momentum.

ADJUSTING YOUR THROWING MOTION. Depending on his position and the circumstance, a player may alter his throwing motion. For example, on longer throws a player should increase his arm swing going back. Rather than pulling his hand out of his glove and bringing his arm straight back, the player may drop his arm down to increase his arm swing, allowing more time and distance to generate greater arm speed. This is recommended for outfielders. They have the longest throws to make, and it's wise to take a fraction of a second longer to increase their arm swing going back. Infielders may also use this on longer throws after backhanding a ball or receiving a cutoff throw from the outfield.

For shorter throws when time is of the essence, players should decrease their arm swing going back. They must get the ball out

From the outfield, the player increases his arm swing to provide more carry for a longer throw. In the infield, time is of the essence, and an infielder often uses a short backswing and throws from different arm angles.

of their glove and immediately elevate their arm as it goes back. Infielders commonly employ this abbreviated backswing on close plays, as do catchers when a base runner is attempting to steal. A catcher who drops his arm down and back to get more on his throw will encounter trouble throwing anyone out.

There also may be times when infielders need to throw the ball from a lower release point. Feeds on double plays, turning a double play off of a low feed, or throwing on the run may force an infielder to throw the ball sidearm or just above or just below sidearm. Because the ball is most often received off the ground, it may take too long to bring the ball up above the shoulder to throw on certain plays. Players must get rid of the ball immediately, and a sidearm delivery facilitates a quicker release. "Players have to show some athleticism to adjust their arm angles and throw on the move," Scott Bradley explains. "Technique can be explained, but to execute the tough plays, players need to trust their athletic instinct."

A crow hop is used by outfielders to gain more velocity and carry on their throws. The crow hop enables a player to maintain or gain momentum on a throw. After fielding a ground ball or catching a fly ball, the player takes a short upward leap off of his glove-side foot. As he leaves the ground, his body turns to align the shoulders and hips with the target. The player lands on his throwing-side foot, steps, and throws. Outfielders should practice this footwork with regularity and use it in game competition.

Methods of Increasing Arm Strength

There are many theories when it comes to devising a plan to increase arm strength. Certain methods work well for some and not as well for others. Many coaches stress the importance of throwing, while others advise players to concentrate their efforts on strengthening the muscles surrounding the throwing arm. There are coaches who restrict weight lifting and only allow flexibility training. Others feel that strength training is imperative to maximizing potential and staying healthy. What is important to the individual player is that his arm-strengthening program is balanced and constructed with individual purpose by a coach or trainer with knowledge and experience.

It would be difficult to find an informed baseball coach or trainer who didn't agree that throwing is essential to building arm strength.

The fast-twitch, slow-twitch, and intermediate-twitch muscle fibers in the throwing arm must be conditioned through repetitious training to reach peak performance. That being said, a player can't just build arm strength by throwing. Throwing is a tearing-down process, so the tissue needs time to recover. Resistance and flexibility training are important as well.

Arm strength is built with some combination of throwing, resistance training, and aerobic/anaerobic training.

—Tom House, former major league pitcher and author

Four Risk Factors in Youth Baseball

The following information was extracted from an interview at the 2005 American Academy of Sports Medicine Conference in San Diego with Dr. James Andrews, cofounder of the Alabama Sports Medicine and Orthopaedic Center. Dr. Andrews has operated on thousands of athletes, including Troy Aikman, Roger Clemens, and Jack Nicklaus, and is an expert in shoulder, knee, and elbow surgery.

- **Year-round baseball**—never giving the throwing arm a complete rest
- **Overuse**—playing in more than one league at the same time.
- **The radar gun**—the constant goal of trying to throw at maximum effort as opposed to throwing correctly
- **Showcases**—players go out to throw hard and show off for a college coach or pro scout when they're not in shape to throw

Andrews adds, "There's a lot that can be done, such as preventive exercises. Even a youth pitcher (or player) needs to be involved in strength training and flexibility exercises for his throwing arm, and of course, there are core exercises for the body."

With the advent of travel baseball and young players competing year-round, the number of arm injuries among youth players has increased exponentially. Much of this is because they are not giving their arms any extended period of rest. Their throwing arms never get to fully recover and rebuild when they're being used 11 to 12 months out of the year. If they're not participating in game competition, it's off-season training. As stated by esteemed orthopedist Frank Jobe, "People forget that young arms need rest."

Major league players don't throw year-round, because they know it's best to "shut it down" for a couple months. Throwing is an unnatural motion to the human body, and the throwing arm needs some time off. The shoulder has very little stability. Some describe the construction of the shoulder as trying to balance a beach ball on the nose of a seal. It's a very intricate joint, and constant throwing without proper rest increases the risk of injury. Players of all ages should build in at least a two- to three-month period during the year when they are not throwing at all.

CORE STRENGTH AND ROTATOR CUFF EXERCISES. Building core strength will improve arm speed and endurance. The legs, hips, lower back, and abdominal regions represent the battery pack for the thrower. Not only will faster hip rotation result in improved arm speed (much like bat speed), but a stronger lower body takes pressure off the throwing arm. This reduces the risk of arm soreness and/or injury. Chapter 3 outlined several core strength exercises that can be used to build arm strength.

Rotator cuff exercises are something a player can do *throughout* the year. It is very important to build up the small muscle groups around the rotator cuff to increase strength and stability in the throwing shoulder. These exercises are highly recommended for baseball players.

A player can perform rotator cuff exercises three or four times a week year-round. He should use three- to five-pound dumbbells or surgical tubing. The player can begin with one set of 10 repetitions for each exercise and build up to three sets of 20 repetitions.

Forward Raises
Position: Stand upright with your knees slightly flexed. Hold the dumbbells down at your sides with your palms faced behind you.

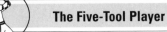
Begin: With your arms remaining straight, raise the dumbbells out in front of you, to shoulder height or just below. Then slowly return to the starting position.

Lateral Raises

Position: Stand upright with your knees slightly flexed. Hold the dumbbells down at your sides with your palms faced inward.

Begin: With your arms remaining straight, raise the dumbbells out to your sides until they reach just beyond shoulder height. Then slowly return to the starting position.

Standing Flies

Position: Stand with your knees flexed and a slight bend at the waist so your back is straight at a 45-degree angle. Hold the dumbbells in toward your midsection with your palms facing inward.

Begin: Keeping your body still and your arms bent, lift the dumbbells upward and back as far as you can. The dumbbells should reach ear height, and your elbows should be at shoulder level. Then slowly return to the starting position.

Rotator Cuff (Prone Position)

Position: Lie face down on a flat bench, and extend one arm to the side. Bend your arm at a 90-degree angle so that your upper arm is parallel to the floor and your hand is hanging with the palm facing behind you.

Begin: Using a lightweight dumbbell, rotate your forearm upward until it becomes parallel to the ground. Then slowly return to the starting position.

Rotator Cuff (Side Position)

Position: Lie on your side on a flat bench. Rest your upper arm on your chest (parallel to the floor) and bent at the elbow at a 90-degree angle so your hand is hanging.

Begin: Using a lightweight dumbbell, rotate your arm upward until it becomes parallel to the ground. Then slowly return to the starting position.

Empty Cans

Position: Stand with both arms down at your sides, hands rotated inward as far as possible with thumbs pointing down.

Rotator cuff exercises (the prone position and the side position) can help prevent and rehabilitate shoulder injuries.

Begin: Keeping your arms straight, slowly raise them forward and slightly out to the sides, as if you were pouring water out of a container. Raise your arms to shoulder height, and then slowly return to the starting position.

LONG TOSS. Long tossing is a popular method of increasing arm strength. A player can long toss three to four times per week during the preseason and continue to long toss during the season. The player may decrease the number of times he long tosses during the season based on the extent of his baseball schedule.

The best time to long toss is at the beginning of practice or before a game. It can be performed at the end of the loosening-up phase

When it comes to shoulder exercises, consult a coach or trainer to make sure you're performing them correctly.

of practice. As a player gets loose, he can begin to stretch out his throws by increasing the distance between him and his partner.

How far a player throws depends on his arm strength. What is important is that the player maintains his mechanics and throws the ball on a straight line to his teammate. If the distance becomes too far to reach his partner in the air on a straight line, he should continue to throw on a straight line but one-bounce his teammate. Players should not begin to tilt their shoulders upward and arc their throws to reach their partner in the air. The proper mechanics must be maintained.

When long tossing, players may get to 90 feet, 120 feet, 150 feet, or even farther. It depends on their arm strength. The most intelligent manner in which to play long toss is to do it with a player of similar arm strength.

UNDERLOADING RESISTANCE TRAINING. Coaches and trainers have suggested the idea of throwing heavier baseballs during the off-season to build arm strength. Throwing 6-, 8-, and 10-ounce baseballs, some feel, will help build up strength in a player's shoulder and help the arm move faster once he throws a regulation 5-ounce baseball. While not saying this type of training is wrong, this book also is not recommending it.

In fact, underloading resistance training is an exercise a pitcher can employ to improve arm speed. Underloading means throwing baseballs that are slightly lighter than a regulation baseball (approximately 4 ounces). This trains the fast-twitch muscles to work at a higher rate of speed. Keep in mind it's the rate of speed the throwing

Long toss is a necessary exercise to improve arm strength.

arm travels that dictates how fast the ball goes. An arm that is literally strong does not increase velocity unless it's moving at a higher rate of speed.

Overcoming a Lack of Arm Strength

The fact that David Eckstein doesn't have an arm that is comparable to Rafael Furcal is not due to lack of effort. And no matter what Johnny Damon does during the off-season, he'll never have an arm like Andruw Jones possesses. Players who lack arm strength must do the little things to maintain their productivity in the field. If they fail to do so, they will experience trouble competing with players who are blessed with stronger arms.

Cal Ripken Jr. was mentioned in the fielding chapter regarding his exceptional ability to anticipate plays. He was able to position himself in areas where the ball was likely to be hit. This allowed him to field the ball sooner and diminished the importance of arm strength. The earlier the ball is fielded, the more time a player has to get the ball to first base.

Ripken was a student on the field before he was an athlete. "I like to learn the hitters and our pitchers and cheat a little bit and cut down the area I have to cover," he once said. "I'm not blessed with the kind of range a lot of shortstops have. The way I have success is by thinking."

Players on the left side of the infield need to position themselves shallower when a fast runner is at the plate. If they play with more depth, the ball is going to take longer to reach them. The runner is gaining ground with each moment, so if the infielder can't rely on his arm to throw the runner out, he's got to get the ball sooner. (Infielders should also move in when the infield grass is high or wet.) Playing a couple steps in shortens the distance of the throw, which assists a player possessing less arm strength.

Outfielders also must shorten their depth to give themselves a chance to throw out a runner who is attempting to score from second base on a base hit. The outfielder needs to factor in the base runner's speed and field condition to determine how much to move in. (The primary factor of field condition is how long or short the grass is cut.) If he stays back, he'll have no shot at the runner.

The path to the ball on the ground must be aggressive. When a player charges the ball, he not only gets the ball in his glove sooner but, as mentioned with infielders, he shortens the distance of the throw. These combined factors make a big difference when a player possesses a below-average arm. The outfielder sprints like a track runner first before breaking down and reaching for the ball with his glove. He should not run with his glove down the entire time, because he can't run as fast that way.

The angle taken to the ball is also important. The player wants to get around the ball first so that his final approach to the ball is on path with the target. Here is a quick example. With nobody out in the ninth inning, the batter hits a hard shot past the third baseman. The batter has good speed and may attempt to stretch it into a double. The left fielder should take a path where he runs forward and to the right. He should take an angle so that he gets around the ball (to its right) and fields it outside his left foot. This will give

Charging the ball hard and getting to it quickly
is a must for players who lack arm strength.

him momentum going toward second base for his throw. He does not want to run a straight line at the ball, intercept it while he's still moving to his right, and then try to make a throw. His momentum will be moving away from the target, and he'll have to stop, plant, and then throw with no momentum. It's difficult to get anything on this throw, especially if the player lacks arm strength. Taking an intelligent path and getting around the ball make a positive difference in how much a player can get on his throw.

Finally, players want to minimize the number of steps they take after receiving the ball and before they release their throw. This is true for all players but is especially important for those with weaker arms. A defensive player should always keep in mind the notion that for every additional step he takes, the base runner is gaining two steps. If a player gets to the ball quickly and gets rids of it quickly, the ball will reach its destination just as fast as a player who has a strong arm but fails to expedite his approach and release.

6
Speed

Speed is the only tool that is used on both sides of the ball. It makes an offensive player more dangerous and a defensive player more electric. The game gets faster at every level of play, and speed is a component that can sometimes make or break the advancement of a player's baseball career.

With speed being the only tool that impacts both offense and defense, a sensible person might assume that it is given considerable attention. However, that is typically not the case. Speed is commonly pushed aside and not viewed as a baseball skill. It's rarely given the respect that the four other tools receive. But speed is extremely important, and players who are developing their game must work on improving this tool to become a better player. Speed affects hitting for average, hitting for power (extra-base hits), baserunning, and defensive play. Not every player has been blessed to run like major leaguer Carl Crawford, but they can improve their speed and overall play. "If you have a choice between power and speed, and it often turns out you have to make that choice, you've got to go for speed," says former major league manager Sparky Anderson.

On the offensive side, a player possessing speed applies pressure to the defense. Routine ground balls afford infielders no margin for error. If they sit back and take their time to ensure that they will field the ball cleanly, a runner motoring down the line may beat the throw. Outfielders are forced to field and return the ball to the infield quickly with fast runners on the base paths. If the outfielder is not quick enough, the runner may take an extra base. Not only will speed win some battles against the defense purely on its own, but the mere presence of a fast runner on base can force mistakes and enable the runner

Speed is the lone tool that helps a player on both offense and defense.

to advance. Says Wake Forest University baseball coach Richard Rembielak, "Speed creates havoc for infielders and disrupts the pitcher's concentration when holding runners. Speed is tough to teach."

Stealing bases, running from first to third on a base hit, and scoring from third base on contact are just some of the game situations where speed becomes an asset. Derek Jeter is a tremendous player. Because he is good at so many things, it often goes unnoticed that he is arguably the best base runner in the major leagues. Speed, explosive first steps, running angles, instinct, and educated risks enhance his offensive talents to a point where he is about as complete a player as they come.

The thing that sets Derek apart is that he's not afraid to fail.

—Charlie Hayes, former Yankees teammate

On the defensive side, speed enables a player to cover more territory, get to the ball quicker, and make plays an individual lacking speed would have no chance to make. As mentioned in Chapter 4, a player can have the greatest hands in the world and a strong, accurate throwing arm to go with it, but if he can't get to the ball in time, those commendable skills are rendered useless. "Without speed, a player is going to be limited to the positions he's able to play," says Colorado Rockies scout Mike Garlotti. "Likely he'll be relegated to corner infield positions [first or third base] or catcher."

Great defensive units don't just make routine plays. They make plays that can change the momentum of a game. For example, when a ball that is crushed to left-center field and destined for extra bases is caught on the run by a fleet-footed center fielder, it's a monumental boost for the defensive team; it's also deflating for the offensive team. Fielding a slow roller, ranging to make a backhand play in the hole, or charging a ground ball to keep the runner from scoring are plays facilitated by speed.

These are all points that outline why speed is one of the five tools, but what can a player really do about his speed? Many athletes,

An outfielder with speed is able to cover more territory. Pitchers love fast outfielders.

coaches, and parents resign themselves to the fact that speed cannot be influenced. "Well, he's slow-footed. Always has been and always will be." That's a terrible mind-set to have and should be one that is unacceptable to a competitive player. Much like arm strength, there are players who enjoy the fruits of physiological makeup. They have a greater number of fast-twitch muscle fibers contacting, resulting in god-given speed. But that by no means condemns a player with mediocre or below-average speed to accept being slow. In fact, those athletes who are less gifted should employ greater focus on running so they can get up to speed.

Improving speed and quickness is an obvious way to play faster. But with that, knowledge in baseball is a great equalizer. Observing and applying information can allow a player to get a better jump, run a direct angle, or start from a better position to get to a ball or base sooner than a player with superior speed. Speed in baseball is not quite comparable to that of what makes a track runner successful. It's more like an obstacle course where you're permitted to cheat if you pay attention to detail.

Baserunning, plyometric training, and agility or speed training are the topics that dominate this chapter. Starting ability and acceleration are also major points of emphasis. Players should put aside their bat, glove, and baseball and pay special attention to the forthcoming information. It may have a greater impact on their game than any other topic addressed in this book.

Speed becomes very disruptive on offense. It commands the attention of the pitcher and the infielders when a fast runner is on base and can influence pitch calling. I've known catchers who will only call for fastballs when a base stealer is aboard. They are thinking selfishly and want the best shot at throwing out the runner if he goes.

—Chris Pittaro, former major league player and director of
pro scouting, Oakland Athletics

Baserunning

Players don't have to be fast to be good base runners. Furthermore, fast runners are not necessarily good base runners. Speed certainly helps, but it doesn't guarantee success on the base paths. Maintaining momentum, aggression, instinct, knowledge of the opponent, and an explosive first step are all pieces of the pie when it comes to effectively running the bases.

Former major league baseball player Dave Gallagher was an excellent base runner. Since his playing days, he has coached in the minor leagues and at college, high school, and youth baseball levels. Gallagher preaches something simple to his base runners that makes perfect sense and also relieves his runners from indecision on the base paths. Gallagher says, "Your base coaches are there only to stop you from running, not to start you." It's a great point, one that breeds aggressiveness on the base paths. If a runner is waiting for the base coach to bring him, it's probably too late to make it to the next base safely. Always assume you're advancing to the next base, and if your coach commands you to put on the brakes, then hold up.

There are two types of running when a player already occupies a base. The first is when the player is running at top speed to get to the next base only. In this case, the base runner is going to take the most direct route possible. This occurs on a ground ball to the infield, attempting to steal a base, tagging up, or running out a force play. The second type is when the player is running at top speed and already has the next base but has thoughts of continuing on to the following base. Here, the runner is going to bend (or bow) out on his approach to the base so he can maintain his momentum and get himself on a direct path to the following base. This happens, for example, on a clean single or an extra-base hit or when the player is trying to score from second base on a base hit.

Rather than address all the fundamentals, short lists of tips for each type of baserunning are provided here:

WHEN RUNNING TO FIRST BASE

- Run straight through the base. Imagine the finish line is five yards beyond first base.
- Don't turn your head to watch the play as you're running. It slows you down.
- Don't leap for the base with your final step. It slows you down, and you risk injury.
- Never slide into first base. It takes longer, and you risk injury.
- Hit the front of the base, not the top or the back.

WHEN RUNNING TO SECOND, THIRD, OR HOME

- From the lead position, make sure you're lined up in a direct path to the base. Don't take a lead off the base from behind it.
- When in doubt, slide!
- On a tag play, pay attention to where the receiver is taking the throw (or where the throw is taking him). If it's going to be a close play, slide to the opposite side of the base from where he's set.

On ground balls to the infield, it's a straight sprint through the base.

- Slide hard into the base if the defensive player is attempting to turn a double play.
- Do *not* slide headfirst into home plate. It's extremely dangerous.
- Don't be content with the base that you're standing on. *Always* think about how you're going to get to the next base.

WHEN MAKING A TURN TOWARD THE NEXT BASE

- Making a turn outward on your approach should happen early enough (about two-thirds of the way) so it's gradual. Think the shape of a banana, not a fishhook.
- Read the play so you can determine as early as possible whether you're continuing to the next base.
- If the play is behind you (for example, if you are running from first to third on a ball hit to the right field), pick up your base coach for assistance. Remember: make your coach stop you, not start you.

- Hit the inside corner of the base in full stride.
- Dip your left shoulder as you hit the base to help align yourself with the next base.

To me, the most valuable speed on the bases is the ability to go two bases at a time—home to second, first to third, or second to home—on a base hit. That really helps generate offense and doesn't require blazing speed but rather other components: an aggressive secondary lead, running good angles, knowing the outfielder's position and arm strength, instinct, and so forth. Stealing bases is great, but it takes everything to go two bases at a time.

—Scott Bradley, former major league player and head baseball coach, Princeton University

---

When running from first to third, the base runner bows out on his path to second base so he can hit the inside of the base and maintain his momentum toward third base.

Professional Scouts' Standard Evaluation for Major League Prospects

60-Yard Dash

6.3–6.5 seconds or less	Exceptional speed
6.6–6.8 seconds	Good speed
6.9–7.0 seconds	Average speed
7.1 seconds or more	Below-average speed

Home to First Base

Left-handed hitter

4.0 seconds or less	Exceptional speed
4.1–4.2 seconds	Good speed
4.3 seconds or more	Average to below-average speed

Right-handed hitter

4.1 seconds or less	Exceptional speed
4.2–4.3 seconds	Good speed
4.4 seconds or more	Average to below-average speed

First to Third Base (or Second to Home Plate)

6.7 seconds or less	Exceptional speed
6.8–6.9 seconds	Good speed
7.0 seconds	Average speed
7.1 seconds or more	Below-average speed

Leads

A base runner increases his chances of advancing to the next base simply by getting a good lead. Remember, a player doesn't have to be fast to be a successful base runner. An aggressive lead shortens the distance to the next base.

A lead that is too short is the more common fault. Base runners tend to play it safe in fear of being picked off rather than gaining every advantage possible to get to the next base. Strange as it may sound, a player who has not been picked off or near picked off during a season is not getting out to a big enough lead.

Base runners should also keep in mind that taking an aggressive lead is to the advantage of the hitter as well. When a runner takes an aggressive lead, it draws the attention of the pitcher. Any degree of focus that is diverted from the batter to the base runner helps the hitter. Perhaps the pitcher concentrates a little less on location and leaves a pitch out over the middle of the plate. Or maybe he rushes a delivery a bit, drags his arm, and hangs a breaking pitch. An active base runner creates problems for the pitcher and defense.

TAKING A LEAD OFF OF FIRST BASE. Once a player has reached first base, his immediate order of business is to pick up the third base coach and check for signs. Don't make the third base coach wait, because it draws more attention to him as he's going through his signs. Next, the runner should quickly turn and check the positions of the infielders and outfielders. Knowing how the defense is positioned (especially the depth of the outfielders) allows the runner to make quick decisions once the batter connects.

When taking a lead, the base runner must keep his eyes on the pitcher. The pitcher has the ball, and once the base runner's eyes leave the player with the ball, the runner becomes vulnerable. In an athletic stance, the base runner should take short steps to the right, leading with the right foot and then following with the left foot. He should count his steps so he has a feel for how far he is from the base. Three steps might be a safe lead. Four steps may be an average lead, and five steps is an aggressive lead. By knowing how far he is from first base through counting steps, the base runner can avoid the mistake of taking his eyes off the pitcher to check his distance from the base.

DON'TS FOR BASE RUNNERS WHEN TAKING A LEAD FROM FIRST BASE

- Don't take your eyes off the pitcher.
- Don't cross your left foot over your right. It puts you in a precarious position to get back to the base.
- Don't bring your feet together as you get out to your lead. It's a poor balance position.

The base runner steps out to a lead and gets set in position.

- Don't jump off the ground when shuffling out to a lead. If the pitcher turns and throws as you leap, you have to first land before you can get back.
- Don't tell the ballpark the steal sign is on. Try to maintain the same mannerisms and disposition with each lead.

In the lead position, the feet are set about a foot outside of shoulder width. The knees are bent, and the rear end is down just above knee height. The hands and arms are held out in front of the midsection so they can be used to assist the runner's explosive first step. The runner is balanced on the balls of his feet with a slight forward lean.

GETTING BACK TO THE BASE. When a pitcher throws over, there are two ways to get back to the base: standing up and diving back on your belly. A base runner should get back standing up when he's taking a safe lead. If he's taking an aggressive lead, he should dive back on his belly.

Getting back to the base standing up is very simple. The runner takes a single crossover step and a leap to the back of the base. His

When getting back to the base standing up, the base runner crosses his right foot over his left foot. Then he leaps off his right foot and reaches for the back of the base with his left foot.

right foot crosses over his left foot, and then he leaps out off his right foot and reaches for the back of the base with his left foot. Once his left foot contacts the base, the runner should swing his body clockwise as he lands so he's facing the next base. This way if the pickoff attempt is overthrown, he can immediately advance to the next base.

When taking an aggressive lead, the runner dives back to the base. As the pitcher initiates his pickoff move, the runner immediately shifts his weight to his left leg. His right leg crosses over

When taking an aggressive lead, the runner should get back to the base on his belly. A crossover step with the right foot is followed by diving back with the right hand. The runner should dive out (not up) to the back of the base.

as he pushes hard off his left leg. The runner extends out with his right arm to the back of the base as he dives. It's important that he remains low to the ground as he dives in, rather than jumping up and out. He should also turn his face to the left as he dives, to protect his face from an errant throw. If he can get back standing up, he can increase his lead.

SECONDARY LEADS. When there is no sign, the base runner breaks into his secondary lead on the pitch. Once the pitcher begins his delivery and it's certain he's making a pitch, the runner takes two or three shuffle steps toward the next base. He should time his shuffle steps so that as the ball is entering the hitting zone, he's landing on his right foot. Now, if the ball is hit, he continues his momentum toward the next base. If the pitch is taken or missed, the runner lands on his right foot, stops his momentum, and pushes off back toward the base.

Advanced base runners pay attention to the flight of the pitch en route to home plate, especially in breaking ball counts. If the runner anticipates a breaking pitch, he can take a more aggressive secondary lead. If the ball looks like it will bounce in the dirt and the runner reads it, he can immediately take off for the next base. Because the catcher has to go down to block the pitch, he'll have a tough time coming up with the ball clean and throwing the runner out from his knees.

Do this a few times to the pitcher during a game, and he'll either stop throwing breaking balls with runners on or, more likely, make sure he doesn't bounce it and hang some up in the zone.

Stealing Bases

An aggressive lead and an explosive first step are important to stealing second base. But part of getting a good jump is breaking at the earliest possible time. Typically, the pitcher's feet are where the runner's eyes should be set. But some right-handers tip that they're going home with the ball before their feet move.

One example of this is when the pitcher rolls his left shoulder inward to initiate the delivery. Once the pitcher turns his shoul-

As the pitch is delivered, the runner shuffles to a secondary lead.

der in, he must go home with the pitch. In this case, there is no need to wait until his left foot picks up for the base runner to take off. Some pitchers rock their weight onto their post leg before lifting their left foot. If the pitcher begins to rock back on his post leg, go!

Holding the glove and the throwing hand high is often an indication the pitcher is throwing over to first base. Also, elevating the throwing elbow while the hand is in the glove is a sign he's throwing to first. When the pitcher holds the glove lower and/or relaxes his throwing elbow, he's likely headed to home plate.

Pay attention to any patterns the pitcher may demonstrate. At times he'll look over once, pick up the catcher's mitt, and go home. If you observe this, take off as soon as his head turns toward home plate. Pitchers are animals of routine. In the heat of competition, many fail to change up their looks and become predictable.

Also, many pitchers have long deliveries to the plate. If the pitcher has a high leg kick from the stretch, take advantage and take off! The catcher's strong arm and quick release time will likely not be enough to compensate for a slow delivery to the plate.

Left-handed pitchers are tougher. If they have a very good move, the best bet for the base runner is to take an educated guess. He should pick a spot where he feels the pitcher is going home and break on first move. That means as soon as the pitcher picks up his right foot, the runner should take off. Nearly every left-handed pitcher has determined if he's going to first or home before he lifts up his leg. Only a minuscule number can see a runner break and then counter with a throw to first.

If a runner is ever picked off breaking on first move, he should keep running without hesitation. He should take a path to the inside of second base and slide directly in. A lot has to happen for the runner to be thrown out. The pitcher has to make an accurate throw to first base. The first baseman must catch the ball, step inside, and make an accurate throw to the shortstop (who may be late covering). The shortstop has to catch the ball and apply a tag in time. The base runner has a better chance of being safe in this scenario than stopping and getting into a rundown.

First Step

The first step is significant when stealing a base. With a lead, the next base is less than 90 feet away, so it's important to get up to top speed as quickly as possible. There are different methods of first steps. A player should make sure his first step is a productive one.

A crossover step (left over right) is the most popular first step. By pushing with the left leg and pulling with the right, the runner crosses his left leg over his right to gain distance and to get the body on a direct path to the next base. The runner should not stand up out of his lead, but rather he should fire low toward the next base.

The upper body can be helpful in generating maximum thrust on that first step. The runner should think about firing his right elbow toward the next base or throwing his left arm across to gain momentum. Every effort is helpful.

Another thought is to go knee-to-knee. The left knee fires inward and the right knee fires out. This immediately gets the body (and feet) in line with the next base.

Whether using a crossover step or starting knee-to-knee, the player must stay relaxed and tension free. Stealing bases is about

The first step is crucial when stealing second base. The runner crosses over (left over right) and uses his upper body to help build momentum.

quickness, and in order for a player to be quick, his body must be in a relaxed state.

It's great to run a good time, but is it usable on the baseball field? I've seen guys run exceptional 60 times but struggle on the field. Can he read the pitcher? Does he get a good jump on the ball? Great speed is only a plus when it can be applied to the field of play.

—Mike Garlotti, scout, Colorado Rockies

Leads and Steals from Second Base

Stealing third base can be easier than stealing second. The base runner is afforded a larger lead, and if he's savvy enough, he can keep his feet moving and have momentum to aid his jump.

Good base runners try to draw as little attention to themselves as possible on second base. They stay calm and quiet and casually edge out to a bigger lead. The key is to keep the feet moving and time the pitcher's delivery to home. Some players will use a walking lead to appear nonchalant and break right into a sprint. Third base is predominantly stolen on the pitcher, not the catcher.

Pitchers are notorious for following the same patterns with a runner on second base. For example, they, glance back at the runner, look home, check back again, and then deliver a pitch home. Most of the time, they're just going through motions with their looks and not really paying much attention to the runner. If the pitcher is a creature of habit, take advantage and get an early jump.

Running Form

Proper technique when hitting or throwing enhances performance. Running is no different. By employing proper running form, a

On second base, the runner wants to draw as little attention as possible. A casual walking lead can give the runner a great jump when stealing third base.

player maximizes his speed on the bases. Ballplayers should have their running form assessed to determine if there are any wrinkles they can iron out that will improve their speed.

First, a player must run relaxed. Much like tension diminishes bat speed and arm speed, it reduces running speed as well. Imagine an Olympic track runner and how his cheeks and jaw bounce and jiggle as he runs. Muscles from head to toe work best when they are free of tension.

Sprinting speed is a balance between stride length and stride frequency. The length of the stride enables the runner to eat up ground, but the strides can't be so long that they stunt momentum. Conversely, it's good to have high-level stride frequency, but not at the expense of having very short strides. The runner's feet may be moving fast, but he's not gaining much ground.

When a player is sprinting, the foot contacts the ground with the outside edge of the ball of the foot. (The faster the runner, the higher the contact point is on the ball of the foot.) As the ball of the foot touches the ground, there is a pushing action. The runner pushes against the ground and springs onto his next step.

If the heel or arch of the foot contacts the ground, it takes time for the ball of the foot to get down and push off to the next step. This time delay is part of what makes many runners slow. Landing on the arch or heel commonly occurs to runners who overstride, are too upright, or lean back as they run. Runners should employ a slight forward lean as they sprint so they're able to land on the balls of their feet and maintain forward momentum in a more aerodynamic position.

Stride length increases with more power from the push-off. By applying more force against the ground, the legs bound farther forward. The stride foot, however, must land under the center of gravity to maintain speed and allow the runner to land on the balls of his feet. Striding too far—where the foot lands out in front of the center of gravity—causes a braking effect. The heel contacts the ground against a stiff front leg, which slows momentum.

The best way to improve stride length is through strength and plyometric training. More powerful, explosive legs enable the runner to apply greater force as the ball of the foot pushes off the ground.

The arms work in opposition of the legs. As the left knee pumps upward, the right arm pumps upward and vice versa. The shoulders are relaxed and square to the direction of the run. The hands rise (relaxed) just above the chin and inside the shoulders. They drop down to the thigh at the bottom of their swing. Coaches often describe this motion to runners as taking their hands from their ear to their back pocket.

The upper body assists in first-step explosion and acceleration during a sprint. Pumping the arms engages the upper body and helps improve stride length and frequency.

Speed and Agility Training

Following is a compilation of sprint drills to improve form and speed. Players can perform these drills prior to pregame, during practice, and individually on their own. Working with a partner or teammate assists in increasing the level of intensity.

- **Down and offs.** The player runs in place, raising knees to waist level. As he runs in place, he emphasizes contacting the ground with the balls of his feet and springing off as quickly as possible. The player should be using his arms as well, raising his left arm up as his right knee elevates and vice versa.

Down and offs

- **Butt kickers.** The player runs forward at a medium pace with a slight forward lean. Each time one of his feet pushes off the ground, he kicks his rear end with the heel of his foot. This emphasizes explosive movement off the ball of the foot and also forces the runner to keep his stride foot underneath his center of gravity.
- **Quick feet.** The player jogs 10 yards. For the next 10 yards, he increases his stride rate and takes as many short steps as possible in that 10-yard interval. His legs move just in front of his body rather than behind or underneath. He jogs another 10 yards and then repeats the short, quick strides. This exercise places emphasis on rapid stride frequency.
- **Lead-hold breaks.** The player gets into the lead position, holds for three seconds, and then breaks. He goes at maximum effort for three or four steps, stops, and then gets reset in the lead position. The purpose of this exercise is to work on making the first few steps as explosive as possible.
- **Catch the crook**. This sprint drill requires two players. One player is seated in the upright position on the ground (or floor). His rear end, feet, and hands are flat to the ground. A

Butt kickers

second player is standing 15 to 20 feet behind him in the lead position. On the call of "Go," the seated player gets up and sprints forward. His teammate behind him also takes off and tries to tag him. This drill is excellent for acceleration and is fun for players. After a few attempts, players should switch positions.

- **The cycle.** Players aspire to hit for the cycle, and practicing running for it helps their chances. Sprint conditioning on the bases enables players to apply their speed work directly to the base paths. Players can practice their angles and maintaining momentum.

  The player first runs out a clean single and makes a turn. He then jogs back to home plate and runs out a double. He jogs back again and legs out a triple before completing the cycle with an inside-the-park home run.

- **Shuffle and switch direction.** The player begins at cone A wearing his glove. Cone B is located 20 feet to his right. In the ready position, the player shuffles to the right until he reaches cone B. Upon reaching cone B, he stops and quickly changes direction to return to cone A.

Sprinting drills can be fun when there's friendly competition.

At the time the player reaches cone B, a coach (or team-mate) hits a ground ball directly at cone A. The player must race to get back to the ball and field it. His goal is to get in front of the ball, but on harder hits, he may have to field the ball on the run. After a few repetitions, the player starts at cone B and reverses the direction of the drill.

- **The hat trick.** The player is set in the ready position facing a coach (or teammate). He is going to attempt to catch three balls in the air and complete the hat trick.

  On the command of "Break," the runner takes a drop step to his right and runs back. The coach throws a ball (approximately 30 yards) over his right shoulder. The player catches the ball on the run and then plants, turns, and throws back to the coach. Next, the player immediately breaks on a straight line to his left. The coach throws a line drive that the player is forced to catch on the run. After the catch, the player stops, aligns himself with his target, and returns a throw to his coach. (A right-handed thrower should use a reverse pivot.) The player immediately sprints directly at the coach. The coach tosses the ball up in the air, forcing the player to catch the ball on the run coming in.

  The goal is to catch all three throws, and the coach (or teammate) should make each catch difficult. After the first set, the player starts off with a drop step to his left to reverse the direction of each catch.

Plyometric Training

Plyometrics refers to exercises that enable a muscle to reach maximum strength in a short period of time. In short, it's speed strength. The two key components to speed strength are starting strength, which is the ability to instantaneously recruit as many muscle fibers as possible; and explosive strength, which is the ability to keep the initial explosion of muscle contraction going over a distance against some resistance.

In baseball, plyometric training is helpful for starting, stopping, accelerating, changing direction, and maintaining balance. These skills are used, for example, when stealing a base, leaping up to make a catch, moving to field a sharp ground ball, tracking down a deep fly ball, and turning a double play.

Following is a series of plyometric exercises. Much like strength training, these specific exercises should not be performed on a daily basis. The muscles need time to recover. Often coaches have players do plyometric training on days they are not strength or speed training. If, for example, a player is in the weight room on Monday, Wednesday, and Friday, then Tuesday and Thursday might be days they incorporate plyometric training.

- **Squat jumps.** The player is set in an athletic position, similar to that of a defensive basketball player. He drops to the squat position and immediately explodes up as high as possible, reaching up with his arms. He lands and returns to the athletic position, ready for his next jump. Three sets of 10 jumps is recommended.
- **Lateral cone jumps.** Standing to one side of a cone, the player is positioned with his feet together. He jumps laterally over the cone to the other side and immediately upon landing jumps back to the starting position. He jumps continuously for 20 jumps and then rests.

Squat jumps

Lateral cone jumps

- **Standing long jumps.** Set in an athletic position, the player swings his arms back and squats before leaping forward as far as possible. He lands, resets himself, and continues to take leaps forward. The player should complete approximately eight jumps in a set or a distance of about 30 yards.
- **Forward/backward lunges.** Standing with both feet together and hands held behind the head, the player steps outward with his left foot approximately two to three feet. As his left foot lands, he sinks down so his right knee nearly touches the ground. He then pushes off his left leg and brings his right foot back alongside the left foot. His next step is with his right foot, and he repeats the process.

  This exercise is not a race. It should be performed slowly. Players should do lunges about 20 yards out, turn around, and continue doing lunges back to the starting position. Remember, it's not a race.

  Backward lunges are precisely the same as forward lunges, except that they're performed moving backward. This is a test of strength and balance.

Forward lunges

- **Lateral squats.** Set in the athletic position, the player takes a lateral step to the right (with his right foot) and squats down as his left foot follows with a step. The athlete should initiate 10 lateral squat steps to the right and follow with 10 lateral squat steps to the left to return to the starting position.
- **Lateral jumps and sprint.** Set four cones 25 yards apart in a vertical line. The player begins at the first cone and performs eight lateral jumps. After completing the eighth jump, he sprints forward to the next cone. He performs eight more lateral jumps and sprints to the next cone. This is continued until he completes his jumps at the final cone.

  A good way to raise the intensity is to set up two lines of cones and have two players race to the finish.

Lateral squats

Top Five All-Time Career Stolen Base Leaders

Rickey Henderson	1,406
Lou Brock	938
Billy Hamilton	912
Ty Cobb	892
Tim Raines	808

Index

About the Author

Mark Gola is the author of several acclaimed baseball books, including *The Louisville Slugger Complete Book of Hitting Faults and Fixes*, *Coaching the Little League Fielder*, *As Koufax Said*, and *The Little League Hitter's Journal*. He was an assistant baseball coach at Rider University and Princeton University and as a player at Rider was a northeast region All-American. Currently, he is the director of hitting at Dave Gallagher's All American Baseball Academy, in Millstone Township, New Jersey. He resides in Robbinsville, New Jersey.